UNIVERSAL
REAL
ESTATE
AGENT

OPERATIONS PROCESS MODEL

A universal guide to building, innovating, renovating, and optimizing your real estate business, from day one through expansion!

TABLE OF CONTENTS

ISBN: 979-8-9915784-4-8 [Print - Paperback]

The Universal Real Estate Agent Operations 'Process' Model presented in this publication are the original intellectual property of Universal Publishing Company, engineered based on experience and expertise in the industry, and are not intended to be construed professional or legal advice. The contents of this book are informational and directional in nature, and the information should not be misconstrued as professional, legal, or tax advice. The author and publisher are not engaged in the provision of legal, tax, or any other additional advisory councils or boards at the time of this publication. This book is a basic comprehensive overview of some of the key pieces and parts of a real estate business, and the author makes no representation, and takes no responsibility for the legalities, rules, laws, and regulations of your business. All rules, laws, and regulations will vary based on your specific location, and it is your duty, and responsibility to clarify all of the local rules, laws and regulations while constructing and conducting your business.

First printing edition 2024

Attention: Copyright Permissions Coordinator
Ureaoperations@Gmail.com

UNIVERSAL LAW OF ATTRACTION:

IN REAL ESTATE, YOUR MINDSET AND ENERGY CAN SIGNIFICANTLY IMPACT YOUR BUSINESS SUCCESS. BY MAINTAINING A POSITIVE OUTLOOK AND FOCUSING ON PROVIDING EXCEPTIONAL SERVICE, YOU ATTRACT CLIENTS WHO SHARE YOUR VALUES AND VISION. THIS ALIGNMENT CAN LEAD TO STRONGER RELATIONSHIPS, INCREASED TRUST, AND A MORE LOYAL CLIENT BASE, ULTIMATELY DRIVING BUSINESS GROWTH.

After reading a simple yet optimistic book, *"Be Useful" by Arnold Schwarzenegger*, I was inspired to find my own way to help others and make a positive impact in the real estate industry. The book emphasizes the importance of using your skills, resources, and influence to contribute to the greater good and make a difference in the lives of others. It encouraged me to look my own stack of skills and success, and think about how I can support and uplift others around me, whether it's through mentorship, education, or creating opportunities for others in the industry. By embodying the principle of being useful, I aim to not only achieve my own goals, but also to help others achieve theirs, and leave a lasting legacy of service and support in my professional industry. Helping you clarify, structure, and build your personal vision of success!

As you embark on the journey of building your real estate business, remember to enjoy the process and stay flexible and open-minded along the way. Having been through this process multiple times for different companies of varying sizes, I can attest that while the steps may be similar, each journey is unique and the outcomes differ. By embracing the journey with a positive mindset, setting good intentions, and remaining open to new possibilities, you can create a fulfilling and successful path forward. Enjoying the process allows you to appreciate the growth, challenges, and victories that come with building a business, while staying flexible and open- minded enables you to adapt to changing circumstances and seize opportunities that may arise.

As you achieve success and stability, it is important to find ways to give back to the community and the industry in a meaningful and impactful way. Whether through mentorship, charitable initiatives, educational programs or industry collaborations, contributing to the betterment of others and the community can not only enrich your own journey but also create a positive impact that extends beyond your business. By finding your own ways to support and give back, supporting charitable causes, or sharing your skills to help others, can bring a sense of purpose and fulfillment, contributing to your overall success and satisfaction in both business and life.

Trust in the journey, stay true to your vision, and let the outcome of success naturally flow as you navigate the exciting and rewarding experience of entrepreneurship! The module pieces and parts of your business – listed throught can be of assistance to someone looking to navigate the real estate industry. These can be helpful whether you're a listing agent, buyer's agent, real estate business owner or aspiring entrepreneur looking to grow your business.

As someone who enjoys building and empowering people, my ultimate goal is to assist individuals in organizing and establishing a solid foundation for their future endeavors, by empowering agents and brokers to scale and grow their businesses effectively and efficiently. My ultimate goal is to enable agents, brokers and owners to *personalize their operations* and gain confidence in every step of the home buying or selling process.

My intention is to encourage you to explore innovative ways to serve your clients and agents authentically, while also leveraging technology to streamline operations. You will maximize your productivity and efficiency by concentrating on the parts of your business that you are passionate about and using technology to automate or outsource the rest. Although creating a business operations manual might be challenging, the process can ultimately be gratifying and pleasurable, making it well worth the effort.

Keep in mind that your business, your process, your vision, your values, and your standards are what will determine your success and have an impact on others who follow you. By embracing this mindset, you can build a sustainable and thriving business that will benefit you as well as your clients, agents, partners, community, and the real estate industry overall.

Building a personalized real estate business model and operations manual can be a challenging and daunting task for many entrepreneurs. One of the key difficulties is that many small businesses often overlook the importance of creating a concrete process. This oversight can hinder their ability to *scale and develop consistency* in the way things are done within their organization. Without a clear and defined process in place, businesses may struggle to maintain quality standards and efficiency in their operations.

Every brokerage or firm will have its unique processes based on its brand identity and local regulations. This diversity in processes can create confusion and inefficiencies, making it difficult for businesses to streamline their operations and achieve a cohesive workflow. Entrepreneurs can establish a set of guidelines and procedures that align with their brand values and ensure consistency in their business practices by creating a personalized business model and operations manual.

Developing a personalized business operations manual not only instills confidence in all facets of the business, but also lays the foundation for long-term success and freedom. Entrepreneurs can ensure that their company runs consistently and effectively by recording procedures, standards, and values early on. This allows them to concentrate on growth and genuine connection. A personalized business operations manual serves as a roadmap for success, guiding real estate agents and entrepreneurs through the complexities of running a business and empowering them to achieve their goals.

Organizing and storing your business processes and information from the outset can significantly ease the process of building and scaling your business in the future. You may increase productivity, guarantee consistency in your procedures, and streamline operations by developing a well-organized framework for your company's operations. This foundation not only facilitates growth but also provides a clear roadmap for expansion and development.

After years of collecting pieces, parts, and information, I have successfully developed a universal real estate agent model that serves as a plug-and-play solution for every agent, team, group, or firm of any size. This comprehensive model streamlines processes, enhances efficiency, and optimizes performance, providing a seamless and standardized approach for real estate agents at any phase of their career. Have you ever been searching for that specific firm document, or the magnet vendor you used once three years ago? Problem solved!

UNIVERSAL LAW OF VIBRATION:

THE ENERGY YOU PROJECT INFLUENCES YOUR BUSINESS ENVIRONMENT. BY MAINTAINING A HIGH VIBRATIONAL STATE, CHARACTERIZED BY POSITIVE THOUGHTS AND EMOTIONS, YOU FOSTER AN ATMOSPHERE OF CREATIVITY AND OPENNESS. THIS ATTRACTS OPPORTUNITIES AND CLIENTS THAT RESONATE WITH YOUR ENTREPRENEURIAL GOALS, HELPING YOU TO INNOVATE AND EXPAND YOUR REAL ESTATE BUSINESS.

UREA OPERATIONS PROCESS **MODEL**

MODULES 1-5

UREA
MODEL

- UREA MODEL | MODULES 1-5
- STANDARDIZE YOUR PROCESS
- STANDARDIZE YOUR SYSTEMS
- OPTIMIZING YOUR OPERATIONS

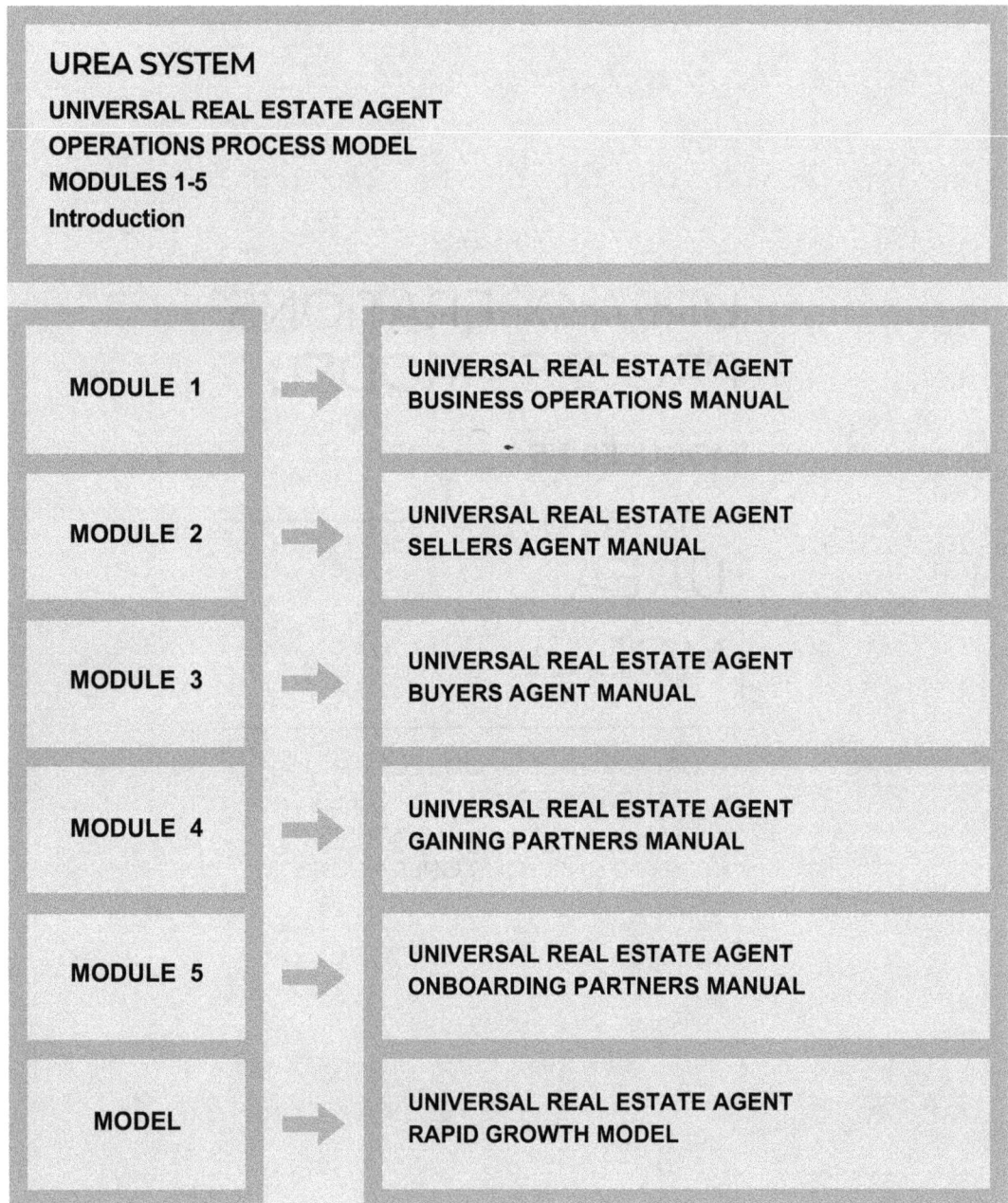

UREA SYSTEM

UNIVERSAL REAL ESTATE AGENT
OPERATIONS PROCESS MODEL
MODULES 1-5
Introduction

MODULE 1	→	**UNIVERSAL REAL ESTATE AGENT BUSINESS OPERATIONS MANUAL**
MODULE 2	→	**UNIVERSAL REAL ESTATE AGENT SELLERS AGENT MANUAL**
MODULE 3	→	**UNIVERSAL REAL ESTATE AGENT BUYERS AGENT MANUAL**
MODULE 4	→	**UNIVERSAL REAL ESTATE AGENT GAINING PARTNERS MANUAL**
MODULE 5	→	**UNIVERSAL REAL ESTATE AGENT ONBOARDING PARTNERS MANUAL**
MODEL	→	**UNIVERSAL REAL ESTATE AGENT RAPID GROWTH MODEL**

This comprehensive guide outlines the core operations, processes, and procedures of your real estate business. It includes information on administrative tasks, financial management, marketing strategies, client communication protocols, and other essential aspects of running your business. A *well-documented business operations manual* ensures consistency, efficiency, and scalability as you expand your business. By thoroughly documenting your process, vision, and expectations for every piece, you can easily identify when or where you may need adjustments or clarification of connections as you grow your business and gain partners.

MODULE 1
UNIVERSAL REAL ESTATE AGENT
BUSINESS OPERATIONS MANUAL STEPS 1-8

STEP 1	**YOUR FOUNDATION	BUSINESS INFORMATION**
STEP 2	**COMPANY CULTURE AND CONNECTIONS**
STEP 3	**MARKETING**
STEP 4	**DOCUMENTS	COORDINATION**
STEP 5	**CUSTOMER RELATIONSHIP MANAGEMENT**
STEP 6	**SOCIAL MEDIA AND TECHNOLOGY**
STEP 7	**PARTNER POSSIBILITIES**
STEP 8	**EXEMPLARY SERVICE**

This manual provides detailed instructions and best practices for agents working with sellers. It covers the listing process, property marketing strategies, pricing strategies, negotiation techniques and closing procedures. By *equipping your agents* with a structured guide, you can ensure that they follow a standardized approach and deliver high-quality service to sellers.

An effective sellers agent manual should be clear, detailed, and concise to ensure optimal engagement and usability. Clarity allows agents to easily understand the procedures and guidelines, while detailed information provides the necessary context and instructions for effective performance. Conciseness helps to eliminate unnecessary jargon and information overload, enabling agents to quickly locate and comprehend the content they need.

**MODULE 2
UNIVERSAL REAL ESTATE AGENT
SELLERS AGENT MANUAL STEPS 1-5**

STEP 1	**SELLERS DISCLOSURE	AGENCY DISCLOSURE: INTRODUCTION FLOW - STEPS 1-10**
STEP 2	**SELLERS DOCUMENTS	PROCESS AND COMPLIANCE: DOCUMENTS	PHASE 1-4**
STEP 3	**TRANSACTION SIDE	SELLERS AGENT: STEPS 1-12**
STEP 4	**STEP BY STEP: SELLERS AGENT: PROCESS + DOCUMENTS - STEPS 1-12**
STEP 5	**STEP BY STEP: SELLERS AGENT	COMMUNICATION OPPORTUNITIES: COMMUNICATION - STEPS 1-8**

Similar to the sellers' agent manual, this guide offers step-by-step instructions for agents working with buyers. It includes information on the home buying process, market analysis, property search strategies, preparation of offers, contract negotiation, and closing procedures. Providing agents with a *clear roadmap for working with buyers* helps them deliver a seamless and professional experience to clients.

An effective buyers agent manual should be clear, detailed, and concise to ensure optimal engagement and usability. Clarity allows agents to easily understand the procedures and guidelines, while detailed information provides the necessary context and instructions for effective performance. Conciseness helps to eliminate unnecessary jargon and information overload, enabling agents to quickly locate and comprehend the content they need.

MODULE 3
UNIVERSAL REAL ESTATE AGENT
BUYERS AGENT MANUAL STEPS 1-5

STEP 1	**BUYERS DISCLOSURE	AGENCY DISCLOSURE:** **INTRODUCTION FLOW - STEPS 1-10**
STEP 2	**BUYERS DOCUMENTS	PROCESS AND COMPLIANCE:** **DOCUMENTS	PHASE 1-4**
STEP 3	**TRANSACTION SIDE	BUYERS AGENT:** **STEPS 1-12**
STEP 4	**STEP BY STEP: BUYERS AGENT:** **PROCESS + DOCUMENTS - STEPS 1-12**
STEP 5	**STEP BY STEP: BUYERS AGENT	COMMUNICATION** **OPPORTUNITIES: COMMUNICATION - STEPS 1-8**

This guide outlines the criteria, process, and strategies for recruiting and selecting strategic partners to support your local real estate business. It includes tips for identifying potential partners, evaluating their qualifications, negotiating agreements, and establishing productive working relationships. You can build a network of reliable and competent partners to enhance your business operations and services by providing agents with a clear roadmap to help them deliver a seamless and professional experience.

To *recruit top talent*, it's essential to demonstrate the value your business offers through comprehensive services and support. By showcasing a strong commitment to agent and partner development, well-being, and a positive work environment, you create an attractive proposition for potential hires. This not only enhances your company's reputation but also signals to candidates that they will be supported in their professional growth, ultimately fostering a culture of excellence and innovation. When top talent sees a clear alignment between their career aspirations and the value your organization provides, they are more likely to join and contribute to your success.

MODULE 4
UNIVERSAL REAL ESTATE AGENT
GAINING PARTNERS MANUAL STEPS 1-5

STEP 1	PARTNER STANDARDS	TALENT REQUIREMENTS
STEP 2	GAINING PARTNERS MANUAL	SERVICE GUIDE
STEP 3	AGENT SAMPLES
STEP 4	PUBLIC PRINT MARKETING SAMPLES
STEP 5	AGENT RELATIONSHIP MANAGEMENT MATERIALS

A comprehensive onboarding process is crucial for integrating new agents into your business or team effectively. This step-by-step guide covers orientation, training, mentorship, goal- setting, performance evaluation and ongoing support for new agents. You can help agents acclimate to your business culture, standards, and practices and set them up for success in their roles by providing a structured onboarding program.

Structuring a *seamless onboarding experience* is crucial for instilling confidence in your business from day one. A well-organized onboarding process helps new employees or agents feel welcomed and supported, allowing them to quickly understand their roles and the company culture. By providing clear expectations, comprehensive training, and accessible resources, you empower newcomers to contribute effectively and feel valued. This initial positive experience not only enhances employee engagement but also fosters long-term loyalty and productivity, ultimately benefiting the organization as a whole.

MODULE 5
UNIVERSAL REAL ESTATE AGENT
ONBOARDING PARTNERS MANUAL STEPS 1-5

STEP 1	AGENT PARTNERED	SIGN DOCUMENTS
STEP 2	AFTER SIGNING	DURING TRANSFER
STEP 3	THE DAY OF TRANSFER	WELCOME!
STEP 4	AFTER ONBOARDING	STEPS FOR ADJUSTMENT

You can facilitate rapid expansion by selecting partners or services that can handle high volume as your business grows. Having a clear vision allows you to map out the necessary steps, timeframe, and costs to reach your goals. With a realistic vision, *well-defined processes* and a solid plan in place, you can efficiently grow your real estate business and potentially expand into other markets. Real estate is an input-output business, meaning that what you invest in terms of effort, resources, and strategy will directly impact the results you achieve. It is crucial to clearly define your vision, set high standards, and establish a sound financial plan to ensure you can set attainable goals and work diligently towards achieving them. By focusing on these key elements, you can position yourself for success and drive your real estate business towards rapid growth and expansion. Think big and set your goals. Then, build a model that can support your vision!

Continue to clarify your vision and goals as you progress through the modules. Keeping your future goals in mind will be a driving force in the decisions and detailed service standards of your business.

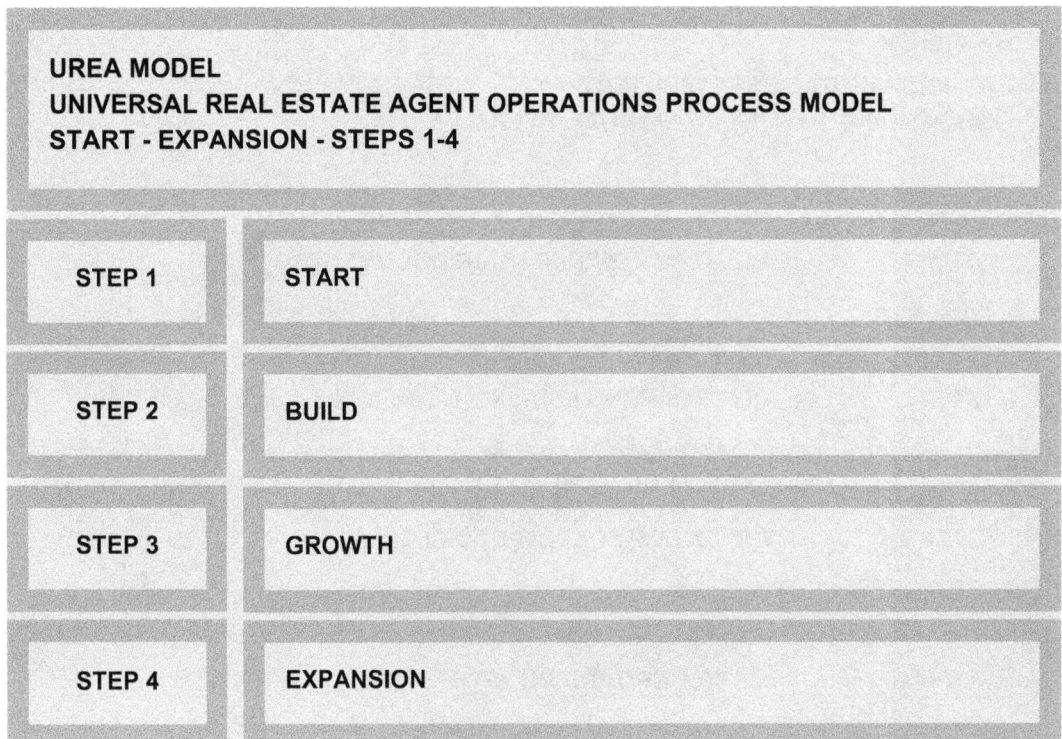

UREA MODEL
UNIVERSAL REAL ESTATE AGENT OPERATIONS PROCESS MODEL
START - EXPANSION - STEPS 1-4

STEP 1	**START**
STEP 2	**BUILD**
STEP 3	**GROWTH**
STEP 4	**EXPANSION**

By *leveraging technology and outsourcing certain tasks*, we can focus on providing true and genuine service to our clients and while consistently servicing at the highest level. Building strong connections within our local community and serving them well is the foundation of a successful real estate business. Through strategic partnerships and efficient systems, we can better serve our customers while reclaiming our time and increasing productivity. Building a personal business book of our services allows us to identify new connection points, streamline processes, and leverage resources to serve our clients, customers, and partners at the highest level. By creating a roadmap for our business operations, we can optimize our workflows, enhance client relationships, and achieve sustainable growth in our businesses.

While many real estate businesses may store their information and documents within their signature platform for convenience and efficiency, it is essential to recognize that additional documents, forms, or templates are necessary to properly serve clients and conduct business effectively and efficiently. These documents may include specific contracts, agreements, disclosures, firm exclusive property listings, market reports, business information and client information, among others. Storing and documenting these essential documents or information in an organized and accessible manner is crucial for maintaining compliance, ensuring transparency and protecting the interests of both the business and its clients. By establishing a systematic approach to managing and storing these documents and information, real estate businesses can streamline their operations, enhance communication with clients, and demonstrate professionalism and accountability in their business practices.

In addition to providing instructional or educational content in an agent manual or e-book, it is highly important to include information about the documents that will be due at specific points or phases in a transaction. This ensures that agents and staff stay compliant with the company/firm's policies, procedures, and legal requirements throughout the transaction process. Individuals involved in the transaction can stay organized, informed, and accountable for completing necessary paperwork accurately and on time by clearly outlining the required documents and deadlines.

Defining your business process in the agent manual or e-book is important for streamlining workflow and training. By documenting and detailing the *steps, guidelines, and best practices* that should be followed in various stages of a transaction, you can establish a standardized approach to handling transactions efficiently and effectively. This not only helps ensure consistency and quality in the services provided but also facilitates training for new agents and staff members by providing a clear roadmap for how transactions should be managed within the firm, company, or business. Ultimately, defining processes in the agent manual or e-book can enhance operational efficiency, improve communication, and support compliance efforts within the real estate business.

People have diverse learning styles, and catering to these preferences can enhance the effectiveness of training and education materials. By creating both a physical agent manual and a digital agent manual, real estate professionals can establish an additional point of connection with their agents as the business grows. An e-book agent manual offers a dynamic and interactive platform that not only optimizes operational processes but also streamlines education and training initiatives. The digital format allows for the inclusion of various elements such as connection points, links, forms, documents, multimedia content, and interactive features, providing a rich and engaging learning experience while creating efficiency for agents. Brokers can leverage the e-book agent manual to empower their firm, company, or business by optimizing the use of information, setting standards, establishing processes, educating agents, and connecting workflow seamlessly. With just a click, agents can access a comprehensive resource that centralizes essential information, facilitates learning, and supports operational efficiency within their real estate business.

By following this step-by-step agent process and adhering to detailed guidelines and regulations for each stage, you can effectively market and sell properties, provide exceptional service to your buyers or sellers, and optimize your real estate business operations. Sustainable success requires clear communication, commitment to high service standards and proper training for all positions within the team, company, business or corporation.

From day one, as an independent broker, part of a team, or a larger firm, company, or business, it is crucial to standardize your systems for success. By integrating, adding, and optimizing any available systems, you can *streamline your operations, enhance efficiency, and set a solid foundation for your business growth*. Here are some key points to consider when standardizing your systems:

Standard Operating Procedures: Develop standardized operating procedures for various aspects of your business, such as client management, marketing, transaction processes, and administrative tasks. Having clear and consistent procedures in place ensures that everyone in your team or firm, company, or business operates in a cohesive manner.

Technology Integration: Utilize technology tools and platforms to automate repetitive tasks, streamline communication, manage client relationships, and track transactions. Implementing a customer relationship management (CRM) system, email marketing software, and other tech solutions can help you work more efficiently and effectively.

Training and Education: Provide ongoing training and education for yourself and your team to stay current with industry trends, best practices, and new technologies. Investing in professional development ensures that everyone is equipped with the knowledge and skills needed to succeed in the real estate industry.

Performance Metrics: Establish key performance indicators (KPIs) to track the performance of your team, firm, company, or business. Monitor metrics such as sales volume, lead conversion rates, client satisfaction, and marketing ROI to identify areas for improvement and make data-driven decisions.

Client Experience: Focus on delivering exceptional service and creating a positive client experience at every moment. Develop processes to ensure timely communication, personalized interactions, and seamless transactions to build trust and loyalty with your clients.

Brand Consistency: Maintain consistency in your branding across all channels, including your website, social media, marketing materials, and client communications. A strong and cohesive brand identity helps differentiate your business and build brand recognition in the market. By standardizing your systems from the beginning and continuously optimizing them as needed, you can create a solid foundation for success as an independent agent or broker.

Embracing technology, investing in training, monitoring performance, prioritizing client experience and maintaining brand consistency are essential components of building a thriving real estate business.

IDENTIFY AND OPTIMIZE

Below is a list of thoughts, questions, and actions that you may need to consider during this process:

- Define your company's mission, vision, and values to guide decision-making and ensure alignment with your goals.
- Develop or create a comprehensive operations manual outlining your company's process, policies, and regulations during the process.
- Identify key performance indicators (KPIs) track and measure the success of your business, and where you may need to adjust.
- Conduct a SWOT analysis to identify strengths, weaknesses, and opportunities.
- Evaluate your current technology stack and consider implementing new tools or systems to streamline operations, and become more efficient.
- Assess your team's skills and training needs to ensure they have the knowledge and resources to succeed.
- Establish clear communication channels and expectations to foster collaboration and transparency within your team.
- Review your marketing and branding strategies to ensure they align with your company's goals and target audience.
- Seek feedback from clients, employees, and stakeholders to continuously improve and optimize your operations.
- Stay informed about industry trends, regulations, and best practices to remain competitive and compliant.
- Delegate tasks and responsibilities effectively to empower your team and maximize efficiency.
- Regularly review and update your operations manual to reflect changes in your business, industry, or market conditions.
- Foster a culture of continuous learning, innovation, and adaptation to drive growth and success.
- Monitor and adjust your operations based on performance data, feedback, and market to stay agile and responsive.
- Collaborate with industry partners, vendors, and experts to leverage their expertise and resources for mutual benefit.

UREA **BUSINESS** OPERATIONS MANUAL

MODULE 1
SECTIONS 1-8

01.

- BUSINESS FOUNDATION INFORMATION
- COMPANY CULTURE AND CONNECTIONS
- MARKETING | PRINT MARKETING
- DOCUMENTS | COORDINATION
- CUSTOMER RELATIONSHIP MANAGEMENT
- TECHNOLOGY AND SOCIAL MEDIA
- SUPPORT STAFF OR PARTNERS
- EXEMPLARY SERVICE
- COLLECT AND CREATE

UNIVERSAL REAL ESTATE AGENT BUSINESS OPERATIONS MANUAL

MODULE 1 | SECTIONS 1-8
Introduction

1.Creating Your Foundation | Business Information: Organizing *business information* is crucial for real estate operations as it ensures that important data and documents are easily accessible and up-to-date, helping to streamline processes and improve efficiency.

2.Company Culture and Connections: Company *culture and connections* play a vital role in real estate operations by fostering a positive and collaborative work environment, enhancing teamwork and communication among team members, and ultimately leading to better outcomes for clients.

3.Marketing: *Marketing* is essential for real estate operations as it helps to promote properties effectively, attract potential buyers or tenants, and establish a strong brand presence in the market.

4.Documents | Coordination: *Documents coordination* is important in real estate operations to ensure that all necessary paperwork is accurately completed and submitted on time, reducing the risk of errors or delays in transactions.

5.Customer Relationship Management [CRM]: *Customer relationship management* is key for real estate operations as it helps to build and maintain strong relationships with clients, leading to repeat business, referrals, and overall satisfaction.

6.Technology and Social Media: *Technology* is a critical component of real estate operations as it enables agents to access property listings, market data, and communication tools efficiently, enhancing productivity and service delivery.

7.Partner Possibilities: Support *staff or partners* are valuable assets in real estate operations as they provide assistance and expertise in various areas, helping to support the overall success of the business.

8.Exemplary Service: *Exemplary service* is essential in real estate operations as it sets the business apart from competitors, builds trust with clients, and leads to positive reviews and referrals, ultimately driving long-term success.

To create a *comprehensive and effective* operations manual for your real estate business, it is essential to break it down into distinct pieces that cover various aspects of your operations. By breaking down your operations into these essential pieces, you create a comprehensive guide that covers all aspects of your business operations. This structured approach not only helps in organizing and standardizing your processes but also ensures that everyone in your organization has access to the information and resources they need to succeed.

MODULE 1
UNIVERSAL REAL ESTATE AGENT OPERATIONS MANUAL
BUSINESS OPERATIONS MANUAL STEPS 1-8

STEP 1	**YOUR FOUNDATION	BUSINESS INFORMATION**
STEP 2	**COMPANY CULTURE AND CONNECTIONS**
STEP 3	**MARKETING**
STEP 4	**DOCUMENTS	COORDINATION**
STEP 5	**CUSTOMER RELATIONSHIP MANAGEMENT**
STEP 6	**SOCIAL MEDIA AND TECHNOLOGY**
STEP 7	**PARTNER POSSIBILITIES**
STEP 8	**EXEMPLARY SERVICE**

UNIVERSAL LAW OF CAUSE AND EFFECT:

EVERY ACTION IN YOUR REAL ESTATE BUSINESS HAS CONSEQUENCES. BY SERVING CLIENTS WITH INTEGRITY AND CARE, YOU CREATE POSITIVE RIPPLE EFFECTS, SUCH AS REFERRALS AND REPEAT BUSINESS. THIS PRINCIPLE ENCOURAGES ETHICAL PRACTICES AND CLIENT-CENTERED SERVICE, WHICH ARE ESSENTIAL FOR LONG-TERM SUCCESS AND REPUTATION BUILDING IN THE INDUSTRY.

BUSINESS OPERATIONS MANUAL

CREATE YOUR FOUNDATION

- CREATING YOUR FOUNDATION
- THE BASICS | CORE VALUES
- MARKET RESEARCH
- IDENTIFY NICHE
- WAYS TO STRUCTURE YOUR BUSINESS
- RULES AND REGULATIONS
- BUSINESS PROJECTIONS | BUSINESS PLAN
- DOCUMENTATION / RECORD KEEPING
- STAY ORGANIZED

01.

MODULE 1 | SECTION 1

YOUR FOUNDATION
[DISCLAIMER]

MODULE 1 | SECTION 1
Introduction

As you navigate the real estate industry, it is crucial to stay informed about the specific *laws and regulations* that govern your area of operation. This includes understanding licensing requirements, contract laws, disclosure obligations, zoning regulations, and other legal considerations that may impact your business practices. By adhering to these regulations, you can *protect yourself*, your clients, and your business from potential legal issues or disciplinary actions.

DISCLAIMER:

BUSINESS OWNERS, AGENTS, AND BROKERS ARE ADVISED TO COMPLY WITH ALL LOCAL, STATE, AND NATIONAL REGULATIONS GOVERNING THEIR INDUSTRY AND OPERATIONS. IT IS THE RESPONSIBILITY OF EACH BUSINESS OWNER TO BE AWARE OF AND ADHERE TO THE LAWS, GUIDELINES, AND REQUIREMENTS SET FORTH BY RELEVANT AUTHORITIES AT THE LOCAL, STATE, AND NATIONAL LEVELS. FAILURE TO COMPLY WITH THESE REGULATIONS MAY END IN LEGAL CONSEQUENCES, FINES, OR PENALTIES.

IT IS RECOMMENDED THAT BUSINESS OWNERS SEEK LEGAL COUNSEL OR CONSULT WITH REGULATORY AGENCIES TO ENSURE FULL COMPLIANCE WITH ALL APPLICABLE LAWS AND REGULATIONS.

1. Define Your Business Model, Firm Model, or Unique Niche: Clearly define your business model idea, including the products or services you will offer, your target market, and your unique selling proposition.

2. Conduct Market Research: Research your industry, competitors, and target market to understand market trends, customer needs, and potential opportunities for growth.

3. Develop a Business Plan: Create a comprehensive business plan outlining your business goals, strategies, financial projections, and marketing plan.

4. Choose a Business Structure: Decide whether to form a company (LLC, corporation) or operate as a sole proprietor as an independent contractor. Consider legal and tax implications when choosing a business structure.

5. Register Your Business: Register your business name, obtain any necessary licenses or permits, and comply with local, state, and federal regulations.

6. Set Up Your Finances: Open a business bank account, set up accounting and bookkeeping systems, and establish a budget for your business expenses.

7. Develop a Marketing Strategy: Create a marketing plan to promote your business, attract customers, and build brand awareness. Utilize online and offline marketing channels to reach your target audience.

8. Build a Professional Network: Establish relationships with suppliers, partners, and industry contacts to support your business growth and success.

9. Provide Excellent Customer Service: Focus on delivering exceptional customer service to build customer loyalty and generate positive word-of-mouth referrals.

10. Stay Compliant: Stay informed about legal and regulatory requirements related to your business, including tax obligations, contracts, and intellectual property rights.

11. Invest in Professional Development: Continuously improve your skills and knowledge through training, workshops, and networking events to stay competitive in your industry.

12. Monitor and Evaluate Performance: Regularly review your business performance, track key metrics, and make adjustments to your strategies to achieve your business goals. By following these guidelines, you can create a successful company or operate as a sole proprietor as an independent contractor, setting yourself up for long term success from the beginning.

By aligning your real estate marketing strategies with your *mission, vision, values, beliefs, and goals*, you can create a cohesive and purpose-driven approach that reflects your business ethos, resonates with your target audience, and drives success in the competitive real estate market.

Your Mission:
Your mission statement defines the purpose and direction of your business, outlining what you aim to achieve and how you plan to serve your clients and community.

Your Vision:
Your vision statement describes your long-term goals, aspirations, and the future you envision for your business. It provides a clear picture of where you want your business to be in the years to come.

Your Values:
Your core values represent the guiding principles and beliefs that shape your business practices, decision-making, and interactions with clients and stakeholders. They reflect the ethical standards and priorities that define your business culture.

Your Beliefs:
Your beliefs encompass your convictions, attitudes, and perspectives on real estate, customer service, and professional conduct. They influence your actions, mindset, and approach to achieving success in the industry.

Your Goals:
Your goals are specific, measurable objectives that you set to drive your business forward, achieve milestones, and fulfill your mission and vision. They provide a roadmap for growth, success, and continuous improvement in your real estate business.

Conducting *in-depth market research* is essential for real estate agents to gain a deep understanding of their local market dynamics, trends, and opportunities. By analyzing market data, trends, and demographics, agents can identify niche markets, unmet needs, or potential problems in their local area that they can address through their services. If you have a better insight into the realities of what the market needs you can really stand out in the market. Buyers and sellers are looking specifically for companies that are highly informed on local market information, trends, and specifics.

Identify Niche Markets:

Market research helps agents identify specific segments of the market that have unique needs or preferences. By specializing in a niche market, agents can differentiate themselves from competitors, target a specific audience, and tailor their services to meet the specialized needs of that market segment.

Fulfill a Need:

Through market research, agents can uncover gaps or unmet needs in the local real estate market. By identifying these opportunities, agents can develop innovative solutions, services, or marketing strategies to address these needs and provide value to clients. Fulfilling a specific need in the market can help agents stand out, attract clients, and build a reputation as a trusted and reliable resource.

Solve a Problem:

Market research can reveal challenges or pain points that clients face in the real estate Process. By understanding these problems, agents can offer solutions, expertise, and support to help clients navigate the complexities of buying or selling a property. By positioning themselves as problem- solvers, agents can build trust, loyalty, and long-term relationships with clients.

In today's competitive real estate market, agents who conduct thorough market research and leverage their findings to create a niche market, fulfill a need, or solve a problem in their local area are better positioned to succeed and thrive. By understanding the unique characteristics and demands of their market, agents can tailor their services, marketing efforts, and client interactions to meet the specific needs of their target audience and establish themselves as trusted and valuable resources in the industry.

Choosing to *build or affiliate* with a brick and mortar brokerage versus a virtual or cloud-based brokerage is a decision that is neither inherently right nor wrong. Each option comes with its own set of unique benefits and advantages. Brick and mortar brokerages offer a physical presence that can create a sense of community and provide a more personal touch for clients and agents. On the other hand, work from home brokerages offer flexibility, scalability, and cost-effectiveness, allowing for remote work and access to a wider pool of talent.

In recent years, due to advancements in technology and increasing availability of virtual assistance services, the real estate industry has witnessed a significant shift towards virtual brokerages and remote work arrangements. Many real estate agents are leveraging virtual platforms, partnering for specialized services, and optimizing their time in more valuable and constructive ways. The traditional need for a physical office and daily in-person connections has largely dissipated, as agents and teams are now able to operate remotely with ease and efficiency.

The rise of virtual brokerages and remote work options has enabled real estate professionals to break free from the constraints of a traditional office setting and embrace a more flexible and agile way of conducting business. Teams, expansion teams, and firms are now able to collaborate and communicate effectively through virtual channels by utilizing technology to streamline operations, enhance productivity, and maintain a strong sense of connection and teamwork.

This shift towards remote work has opened up new opportunities for solo entrepreneurs and independent agents to grow their businesses at rapid rates by tapping into a vast network of connections and resources at their fingertips. With the ability to access virtual assistance, specialized services, and networking opportunities online, solo entrepreneurs can expand their reach, increase their efficiency, and scale their businesses more effectively than ever before. This trend towards remote work and virtual collaboration is transforming the real estate industry, empowering agents to work smarter, connect with clients and partners globally, and achieve greater success in a rapidly evolving virtual world.

Once the decision is made to go with either a brick and mortar, virtual, or cloud-based brokerage, it is crucial to *document* the details of the business model, services offered, operational processes, and key partnerships. It may be necessary to add services, vendors and partnerships of your own to personalize your business. By documenting these details, you can ensure clarity, consistency, efficiency in your operations, and set a solid foundation for the success and growth of your business.

Types of Ownership:

- When setting up a business, you also need to consider the different types of ownership and entities available. Sole proprietorships, partnerships, corporations, and limited liability companies (LLCs) are some of the common forms of ownership. Each type has its own advantages and disadvantages in terms of liability, taxation, and management structure. It is important to choose the right form of ownership that best suits your business needs.

Insurance:

- Property insurance, business insurance, and omissions insurance are essential for real estate businesses. Property insurance protects your physical assets, such as buildings and equipment, from damage or loss. Business insurance provides coverage for liability claims, property damage, and other risks associated with running a business. Omissions insurance protects you from claims of negligence or errors in your professional services.

Capital:

- Working capital is the amount of money needed to cover the day-to-day operations of a business. Projections, on the other hand, are estimates of future financial performance based on historical data and market trends. Working capital and projections are closely connected, as accurate projections help you determine how much working capital you need to keep your business running smoothly.

Commission Standards:

- When creating commission standards for your business, Or looking to build a business with a firm, company, team or group you need to consider factors such as capping, structure, and decision-making. Capping refers to setting a limit on the amount of commission an employee or agent can earn or will pay to the firm, company, team or group, while structure involves defining the commission rates and payment terms. Decisions need to be made on how commissions will be calculated, distributed, and monitored to ensure fairness and transparency in your Individual team or business when you choose to build, grow, and expand.

One important aspect of creating a business plan is to check your *local regulations*. It is crucial to understand the laws and regulations that govern businesses, and real estate in your local area, as they can have a significant impact on your operations. Failure to comply with local regulations can result in fines, penalties, or even the closure of your business.

Creating a business entity and ensuring compliance with municipal regulations are essential steps in establishing a legal and legitimate business operation. To start, you will need to choose a suitable business structure, such as a sole proprietorship, partnership, limited liability company (LLC), or corporation. Each structure has its own legal and tax implications, so it is important to carefully consider which one aligns best with your business goals and needs.

Creating a business entity and ensuring compliance with municipal regulations are critical steps in establishing a successful and legally sound business. By taking the time to research and understand the requirements for operating a business in your municipality, you can set a solid foundation for your business and avoid potential legal and regulatory pitfalls in the future.

When considering your business in the real estate industry, it is essential to think about it in levels or types of agency to determine the structure and dynamics of your operation. Each part represents a distinct scenario that may apply to your situation. You may also affiliate with a firm, company, team or group with a goal to build your own business, team, or company. While building your business, keep in mind all the things that you may offer or do differently, and services you may add to grow or scale your business quickly.

By understanding which category your real estate business falls into, you can better assess your strengths, challenges, and opportunities for growth. This awareness will help you tailor your strategies, processes, and goals to align with the specific dynamics of your business structure, ultimately leading to a more successful and sustainable operation in the real estate industry.

1. Solo Real Estate Business: If you own a solo real estate business, you are operating independently as a single entity. This means that you are solely responsible for all aspects of your business, from client acquisition to transaction management. As a solo business owner, you have full control over decision-making and business operations while following rules and regulations, but you may also face challenges such as limited resources and scalability.

2. Group or Team Owner Under a Larger Firm:
If you are the owner of a group or team operating under a larger real estate firm, you are collaborating with other agents or professionals within a larger organization. This structure allows for shared resources, support, and potentially access to a broader client base. Working under a parent firm provides a sense of community and shared goals, but it also comes with guidelines and policies set by the overarching entity.

3. Affiliated Agent | Firm or Team:
As an individual agent on a team or an independent agent working for a firm, you have the flexibility of operating within an established organization while maintaining some level of autonomy. You may benefit from the resources and brand recognition of the firm, as well as the support and collaboration of a team. However, you must also adhere to the firm's guidelines and work within their established framework.

4. Large Team | Franchise or Firm Owner:
As a real estate team, franchise or firm owner, there are numerous moving pieces and parts that require careful management and coordination to ensure smooth operations and success. These moving components may include multiple agents and brokers, various properties and listings, client relationships, marketing and advertising strategies, financial transactions, legal compliance, technology systems, administrative tasks, and more.

An independent agent *affiliated* with a larger real estate firm, company, team or group may have a unique set of roles and responsibilities that can vary based on the specific affiliation and the services offered by the larger entity. Some of the general responsibilities of an independent agent in this scenario may include:

Representing a Larger Entity: As an independent agent affiliated with a larger entity you may be responsible for representing the brand and upholding the values and standards set by the larger entity. This may include adhering to company policies, branding guidelines, and ethical standards in all business dealings.

Leveraging Firm, Company, Group, or Team Resources: Independent agents can benefit from the resources and support offered by the larger entity, such as training programs, marketing materials, technology platforms, and administrative assistance. It is important for the independent agent or broker to effectively utilize these resources to enhance their business operations and provide better service to clients.

Affiliated Agent Collaboration: Independent agents may work closely with other agents within the larger entity to share knowledge, best practices, and leads. Collaboration with other agents can help expand your network, generate referrals, and create opportunities for cooperation on transactions.

Customizing Services: Depending on the affiliation with the larger entity, an independent agent may have the flexibility to customize services to meet the specific needs of their clients. This may involve offering additional services, specialized expertise, or unique marketing strategies to differentiate your brand and attract clients.

Outsourcing or Substituting Services: Independent agents may choose to outsource or substitute certain services to accommodate their brand and meet client demands. This could include partnering with third-party vendors for marketing, photography, staging, or other specialized services to enhance the client experience and streamline operations.

Overall, the roles and responsibilities of an independent agent affiliated with a larger entity can be diverse and may require flexibility, adaptability, and a strong understanding of the overseeing entity 's services and brand. By effectively leveraging resources, collaborating with other agents, customizing services, and outsourcing or substituting services as needed, independent agents can create a successful business model that aligns with their brand and meets the needs of their clients.

As an *independent agent or business owner*, it is essential to be self-motivated, organized, and proactive in managing all aspects of your business. Building a strong network, providing excellent service to clients, and staying current with industry trends can help you succeed as an independent real estate agent. Rules and regulations of working as a solo agent or broker will vary depending on your location, and you may need to go through various extra steps to build your local business, such as level of production, education, or fees.

An independent real estate agent / owner who is not affiliated with a brokerage or team has the flexibility to operate their business independently, while following rules and regulations. Some of the roles, responsibilities, and tasks that an independent agent, or real estate business owner may need to perform include:

Technology and Tools: Utilizing real estate technology platforms, tools, and resources to streamline operations, market properties, and communicate with clients.

Business Operations: Managing all aspects of their real estate business, including setting goals, developing business plans, and overseeing day-to-day activities.

Marketing and Branding: Developing and implementing marketing strategies to promote themselves and attract clients, as well as building a strong personal brand identity.

Client Services: Providing high-quality service to clients, including assisting with buying, selling, or renting properties, negotiating deals, and guiding clients through the transaction process.

Financial Management: Handling financial aspects of the business, such as budgeting, accounting, and managing cash flow.

Compliance: Ensuring compliance with real estate laws and regulations, as well as industry standards and ethics.

Networking and Lead Generation: Building relationships with potential clients, referral sources, and industry partners to generate leads and grow their business.

Continuing Education: Staying informed about market trends, industry developments, and best practices through ongoing education and professional development.

Administrative Tasks: Handling administrative duties such as maintaining client records, scheduling appointments, and managing paperwork related to transactions.

Legal and Contractual Responsibilities: Understanding and executing legal contracts, disclosures, and other documents required for real estate transactions.

Creating a *business projections* sheet involves forecasting the financial performance of a business over a specific period of time. This sheet helps brokers, business owners, and stakeholders understand the potential revenue, expenses, and profitability of the company. Here are some key elements that may be included in a business projections sheet:

1.**Revenue Projections:** This is calculated by subtracting the COGS from the total revenue. It represents the profit generated from the core business activities before considering other expenses.

2.**Cost of Goods Sold (COGS):** This is the final profit figure after deducting all expenses, including operating costs, taxes, interest, and depreciation. It indicates the overall profitability of the business.

3.**Operating Expenses:** This section covers the general operating costs of the business, such as rent, utilities, salaries, marketing expenses, insurance, and office supplies.

4.**Gross Profit:** This section outlines the expected sales and revenue generated by the business It may include detailed breakdowns of revenue sources, such as product sales, services, subscriptions, or advertising.

 5.**Net Profit:** This section includes the direct costs associated with producing goods or delivering services. It may include expenses such as paid commissions, marketing vendors, and support partners.

6.**Cash Flow Projections:** This involves testing the impact of different scenarios on the financial projections, such as changes in sales volume, pricing, or costs. It helps in assessing the business' resilience to potential risks.

7.**Break-Even Analysis:** This analysis determines the point at which the business' total revenue equals its total expenses, resulting in neither profit nor loss. It helps in understanding the minimum sales required to cover costs.

8.**Assumptions:** It is essential to document the assumptions made while creating the projections sheet, such as market trends, pricing strategies, growth rates, and cost estimates.

9.**Sensitivity Analysis:** This section forecasts the inflow and outflow of cash over a specific period. It helps in understanding the liquidity and financial health of the business.

10.**Summary and Conclusion:** This section provides a concise overview of the projected financial performance, highlighting key metrics, trends, and potential areas of concern or opportunity.

Creating a business plan is an essential step in starting a new business or expanding an existing one. A *well-thought-out business plan* serves as a roadmap for your business, outlining your goals, strategies, and financial projections. It helps you stay focused and organized, and provides a clear direction for your business. Let your vision define the following by setting a goal of where you want to be, understanding the resources it will take to accomplish the goal, and create a process that will work for your vision. Documenting your finances, and partnering the proper financial support such as an accountant can be vital from start to expansion. Partnering with an accountant or accounting firm that can grow with your real estate business is ideal.

1.Finances:

Operating costs of a business refer to the expenses incurred in the day-to-day operations of a company. This can include costs such as rent, utilities, salaries, supplies, insurance, and maintenance. Operating costs are essential for the functioning of the business and are subtracted from the revenue generated to calculate the company's profit. Understand your working capital, and plan accordingly.

2. Fees:

In real estate, there are various fees that agents and brokers need to consider when conducting transactions. These fees can include technology fees for software and tools used in the industry, marketing expenses for promoting properties, client appreciation costs for maintaining relationships with clients, and agent appreciation costs for recognizing and rewarding the efforts of agents. These fees are important to factor in when determining the overall cost of doing business in the real estate industry.

3.Profit:

Gross profit is the total revenue generated by a business minus the cost of goods sold. This provides a basic measure of a company's profitability before accounting for other expenses. Net profit, on the other hand, is the total revenue minus all expenses, including operating costs, taxes, and interest. Net profit is a more comprehensive measure of a company's profitability as it takes into account all expenses incurred in the business operations. Loss occurs when the total expenses exceed the total revenue, resulting in a negative net profit.

Record keeping is a crucial aspect of running a successful real estate business. Keeping accurate and up-to-date records helps you track your finances, monitor your performance, and comply with legal and regulatory requirements. In the real estate industry, there are specific items that need to be *recorded and tracked* on a regular basis to ensure the smooth operation of your business.

Daily Record Keeping Involves documenting all transactions, interactions, and activities that occur on a daily basis. This includes keeping track of client meetings, property showings, phone calls, emails, and any other tasks related to your real estate business. Daily record keeping helps you stay organized and ensures that you do not miss any important details or deadlines.

Weekly Record Keeping Involves reviewing and summarizing your daily records at the end of each week. This allows you to track your progress, identify any trends or patterns, and make any necessary adjustments to your business strategies. Weekly record keeping also helps you stay on top of your tasks and priorities, ensuring that you stay focused and productive.

Monthly Record Keeping Involves reconciling your financial statements, tracking your income and expenses, and analyzing your overall performance for the month. This helps you identify any areas of improvement, make informed decisions, and plan for the future. Monthly record keeping also helps you prepare for tax season and ensures that you are compliant with financial reporting requirements.

Quarterly Record Keeping Involves reviewing your financial statements, analyzing your business performance, and setting goals for the next quarter. This allows you to track your progress, make adjustments to your strategies, and stay on track with your business objectives. Quarterly record keeping also helps you identify any potential issues or opportunities that may arise in the future.

Yearly Record Keeping: By maintaining organized records, owners can track their financial performance, identify trends, and make strategic adjustments to optimize their business operations. Additionally, thorough record keeping can help demonstrate compliance with regulatory requirements, provide insights into the financial health of the business, and streamline annual reporting processes. Overall, yearly record keeping is crucial for business owners to effectively manage their finances, assess their business performance, and plan for future growth.

Organizing and storing your legal, tax information, licenses, permits, and other compliance regulations is crucial for the long-term success and sustainability of your business. Keeping these documents in order helps ensure that you are operating *legally and ethically*, and can protect your business in the event of disputes, audits, or insurance claims. Here are some reasons why organizing and storing these documents is important:

1. Compliance: By maintaining up-to-date licenses, permits, and compliance regulations, you demonstrate that your business is operating within the legal framework set by regulatory authorities. Failure to comply with these requirements can result in fines, penalties, or even the closure of your business.

2. Tax Obligations: Properly organizing and storing your tax information, such as financial records, receipts, and tax returns, is essential for accurate reporting and filing of taxes. In the event of an audit, having organized tax records can help you provide the necessary documentation to support your tax filings.

3. Insurance Claims: In the event of a disaster or unforeseen event that results in damage to your physical location, having organized legal and insurance documents can help expedite the claims process. This includes property insurance, liability insurance, and any other relevant insurance policies that may be needed to cover losses.

4. Business Transactions: When seeking financing, partnerships, or potential acquisitions, organized legal and compliance documents can provide transparency and credibility to potential investors or partners. Having these documents readily available can help facilitate due diligence processes and negotiations.

5. Future Growth: As your business grows and evolves, having organized legal and compliance documents can help you navigate regulatory changes, expansions into new markets, or the introduction of new products or services. It can also help you identify any gaps or areas of improvement in your compliance efforts.

Organizing and storing your legal, tax information, licenses, permits, and other compliance regulations is essential for maintaining the integrity and legality of your business operations. These documents can also be valuable in protecting your business interests, supporting insurance claims, and facilitating future growth and expansion. It is important to establish a system for organizing and storing these documents securely, whether in physical or digital format, to ensure easy access and retrieval when needed.

FOUNDATION | BUSINESS INFORMATION

MODULE 1 | SECTION 1
Conclusion

FINANCIALS:
BUSINESS BANKING ...

Having a business banking account is crucial for a real estate business as it helps to separate personal and business finances, track expenses and income, and build a credit history for the business. Additionally, having a separate trust account for holding client funds is required by law in many states to ensure the protection of client funds. Some other banking accounts that may be necessary for a real estate business include a payroll account for managing employee salaries, a merchant account for processing credit card payments, and a business savings account for setting aside funds for taxes or emergencies. When setting up and managing business banking accounts, it is important to keep your business information handy. Make sure you are fully aware of the types of accounts you will need to properly operate your personal real estate business.

CORE BUSINESS INFORMATION:
ASK YOURSELF...

Writing down your mission, vision, values, beliefs, and goals is a powerful exercise that can provide clarity and direction for your real estate business. When you have a clear understanding of your mission, vision, values, beliefs, and goals, you can focus your efforts on building systems and processes that align with these principles.

- What is your business, affiliation, or structure?
- Type of brokerage?
- Brick and Mortar / or Remote?
- What type of business are you building?
- What is your niche?
- Is this a sole prop, LLC, Corp, Ect?
- Have you organized your legal, tax, and business information?
- Have you set up your business banking accounts if needed?
- What is your projected income?
- What are your projected expenses?
- What are your financial projections? Month, quarter, year?

BUSINESS OPERATIONS MANUAL

CULTURE AND CONNECTIONS

- CREATE YOUR CULTURE AND CONNECTIONS
- THE VALUE OF CULTURE AND CONNECTIONS
- CREATING YOUR CONNECTIONS
- KNOWLEDGEABLE CONNECTIONS
- VENDOR CONTACT STORAGE PIECE
- ITEM AND INVENTORY STORAGE
- CREATE YOUR CONTACT STORAGE TEMPLATES

02.

MODULE 1 | SECTION 2

CREATE YOUR CULTURE AND CONNECTIONS

SECTION 2
Introduction

Aligning your culture and connections with your company's vision and values is not just a strategic advantage, it is imperative for long-term success. When a company's internal culture resonates with its external messaging and goals, it creates a cohesive environment where employees are more engaged, motivated, and aligned with the organization's objectives. This *synergy* fosters a sense of belonging and purpose, enabling teams to work collaboratively towards common goals. When employees, clients, and partners believe in the *vision and values* of the company, they become ambassadors of the brand, which enhances customer loyalty and strengthens the overall market position.

As organizations scale, the complexity of maintaining this alignment increases. It becomes essential to partner with *efficient collaborators* who can adapt and grow alongside your vision. These partners can help ensure that as the company or business expands, the core values and culture remain intact. By leveraging expertise from partners who understand your brand and can implement strategies that align with your vision, you create a framework for consistency, efficiency, and effectiveness. This not only preserves your brand identity but also amplifies its impact in the marketplace.

Strategic partnerships can facilitate the sharing of best practices and resources, enabling your company to respond more effectively to changing market dynamics. This adaptability is crucial in today's fast-paced business environment, where customer expectations and technological advancements are constantly evolving. By working with partners who can scale with your vision, you ensure that your company remains agile and responsive, while also maintaining the integrity of your brand. Ultimately, this alignment between culture, connections, and company values is foundational for sustainable growth and long-term success.

THE VALUE OF CULTURE AND CONNECTIONS

Enhanced Teamwork:

- A culture of collaboration through connections encourages employees to work together, share ideas, and leverage each other's strengths to achieve common goals. When team members collaborate effectively, and share connections, they can accomplish more and produce better results. Connection is key.

Improved Problem-Solving:

- Open communication allows for the free exchange of ideas and perspectives, leading to more creative and effective problem-solving. When employees feel comfortable sharing their thoughts and opinions, they can collectively come up with innovative solutions to challenges.

Increased Employee Engagement:

- Valuing partner input and creating a collaborative culture can boost employee morale and engagement. When employees feel that their contributions are valued and their voices are heard, they are more likely to feel motivated and committed to their work.

Innovation and Creativity:

- Collaboration and open communication foster a culture of innovation and creativity within the organization. Companies can drive innovation and stay ahead of the competition by encouraging employees to share ideas and think outside the box.

Stronger Relationships:

- Building a culture of collaboration and open communication helps strengthen relationships among team members, partners, and stakeholders. Trust and mutual respect are essential for effective collaboration and can lead to stronger, more productive working relationships.

Adaptability and Resilience:

- A culture that values partner input and encourages collaboration enables organizations to be more adaptable and resilient in the face of change. By working together and sharing knowledge, companies can navigate challenges and seize opportunities more effectively.

Alignment | Vision and Values:
- Partnering with individuals and companies that share your vision and values helps create a cohesive and unified approach to business. It ensures that all parties are working towards common goals and objectives, fostering a sense of collaboration and mutual respect.

Operational Efficiency:
- Working with reliable and reputable partners can streamline operations, improve efficiency, and enhance the overall performance of your business. By choosing partners who deliver quality services and products, you can ensure that your operations run smoothly and effectively.

Reputation Management:
- Your choice of partners reflects on your company's reputation and credibility. Selecting partners who uphold high standards of professionalism, integrity, and ethical conduct can enhance your reputation in the industry and build trust with clients and stakeholders.

Community Engagement:
- Connecting with your local community through partnerships, sponsorships, and collaborations not only creates direct connections within the community but also helps establish a healthy local referral market. By supporting local businesses and organizations, you can build relationships, generate referrals, and strengthen your presence in the community. To support your local market and referrals, it is important to create a local vendor list of basic needed contacts for every individual business, team, or firm.

Having a basic understanding of the *product you are selling*, such as a house is essential for real estate agents to appear knowledgeable and trustworthy to potential buyers. By gaining knowledge about various home systems and structural components, agents can effectively communicate with clients, address their questions and concerns, and give valuable insights during the property viewing and negotiation process. This knowledge not only instills confidence in clients but also helps agents identify potential issues or opportunities for improvement in the homes they are selling.

BASIC HOME SYSTEMS:
1. HVAC (Heating, Ventilation, and Air Conditioning) system
2. Plumbing system
3. Electrical system
4. Roofing system
5. Insulation system
6. Foundation system
7. Septic system (if applicable)
8. Security system
9. Water heating system
10. Appliance systems (e.g., kitchen appliances, washer/dryer)

BASIC STRUCTURAL COMPONENTS:
1. Foundation: The base structure that supports the entire house
2. Walls: Vertical structures that divide and enclose the living spaces
3. Roof: The top covering of the house that protects it from the elements
4. Windows: Openings in the walls that allow light and air to enter
5. Doors: Entry and exit points to the house
6. Flooring: The surface on which people walk inside the house
7. Ceilings: The upper interior surface of a room
8. Framing: The framework that provides structural support to the house
9. Siding: The exterior cladding material that protects the house
10. Gutters and downspouts: Systems that collect and divert rainwater away from the house

By familiarizing themselves with these basic home systems and structural components, real estate agents can better understand the properties they are selling and effectively communicate with buyers, leading to successful transactions.

STORE YOUR CONTACTS

VENDOR SERVICE PROVIDER [TYPE] EXAMPLE: [INSPECTOR, PAINTER, ECT]

For each VENDOR CONTACT you will need to use regularly for your business / Attach: Information and details:

- Company Name
- Name of Contact or Service
- Contact / Provider
- Phone / Email
- Website
- Provider Notes
- Link to Platform / Website / or Both

Spread Sheet Example Below:

SERVICE/ VENDOR	COMPANY	CONTACT	PHONE/EMAIL		WEBSITE	NOTES	LINKS OR CONNECTION
HOME INSPECTIONS	QRP INSPECT	JIM SMITH	# 000-000-0000 JIM@QRP.COM		QRPINSPECT.COM	BOOK ONLINE	QRPINSP.COM /ORDER LOGIN / PASS...

SERVICE OR PLATFORM EXAMPLE: [CRM, MLS, MARKETING]

For each PLATFORM OR SERVICE PROVIDER you will need to use regularly for your business / Attach: Information and details

Spread Sheet Example Below:

SERVICE	PAYMENT PLAN	WHO WILL PAY	COST OF SERVICE	COMPANY	CONTACT	PHONE/EMAIL	WEBSITE	NOTES	LINKS OR CONNECTION
CRM PLATFORM	MONTHLY	AGENT: FIRM:	AGENT:$ FIRM:$$	QRP CRM SERVICE	JIM SMITH	# 000-000-0000 JIM@QRP.COM	QRPCRM. COM	DRAFT 1ST OF THE MONTH	QRPCRM. COM/LOGIN ATTACH: LOGIN / PASS

ITEM AND INVENTORY INFORMATION

For Each Item you will need to KEEP IN INVENTORY / purchase, or rent for your business / Attach: Contact Information and details

1. Item
2. Company
3. Contact Information / Person
4. Phone - Email - Company page Link
5. Ordering Notes - Instructions
6. Preferred Ordering Quantity
7. Responsible Party / Position to Order
8. Price / Cost
9. Responsible Party [Payment] / Agent or Business

Spread Sheet Example Below:

ITEM	COMPANY	CONTACT	PHONE/EMAIL WEBSITE	NOTES	LINKS OR CONNECT	PRICE / COST	ORDER QTY	PARTY TO ORDER	PARTY TO PAY
BRANDED NOTEPADS 8.5 X 11	QRP BRANDING	JIM SMITH	# 000-000-0000 JIM@QRP.COM QRPBRAND.COM	ORDER BULK ONLINE	QRPBRAND.COM /ORDER LOGIN / PASS	AGENT: BUSINESS:	MINIMUM OF 50	AGENT: BUSINESS: ADMIN: ECT...	BUSINESS: WILL PAY FOR BULK, AND PASS DISCOUNT TO AGENT,

For Each Item you will need to KEEP IN INVENTORY/ purchase, or rent for your business [Copy the item contact information and details list / or combine the information]. You may choose to keep your inventory information attached to your ordering information and details. How you choose to store and organize is your personal preference. Organize: Inventory Information:

- Item
- Business / Company Cost
- Agent Price
- When to order
- Quantity in stock
- Reference / SKU or QR code
- Order Link

Spread Sheet Example Below:

SERVICE	BUSINESS COST BULK	AGENT PRICE EACH	QTY IN STOCK	ORDER + QTY	ITEM REFERENCE SKU / QR	ORDER LINK
BRANDED NOTEPADS 8.5 X 11	$$$	$$$	X AMOUNT	QTY OF 50 FIRST OF THE MONTH, BIWEEKLY, ECT.	0000-000-00	QRPBRAND.COM/ORDER LOGIN / PASS

CULTURE AND CONNECTIONS
MODULE 1 | SECTION 2
Conclusion

MANAGE YOUR CONNECTIONS...

Building your contacts is building your business! Compile a list of service providers you may need throughout a transaction. Start to collect vendors, and service providers, so you are best equipped to help your buyer or seller with their property needs. This will also help you build local relationships, and add value to your business. It is always advised to recommend three service providers for any services offered to your clients by outside vendors to add value, ultimately letting the client choose which provider may work best for them.

ASK YOURSELF...

- Have you compiled a list of your company property vendors?
- Do you have a list of knowledgable connections for your business?
- Have you collected your business contacts? Attorney, accountant, ect?
- Do you have a list of inventory you will regularly use for your business?
- Do you have a niche? Have you listed your niche contacts?
- How will you service your business, clients, and partners? List any service contacts for your business.

BUSINESS OPERATIONS MANUAL

MARKETING

- BUILD YOUR BRAND
- BUSINESS BRANDING
- BUILD YOUR COMPREHENSIVE MARKETING PLAN
- BUSINESS BRANDING | MARKET YOUR LISTINGS | SIGNS
- TYPES OF REAL ESTATE MARKETING
- FIRM TO AGENT MARKETING
- AGENT TO PUBLIC MARKETING
- COMPREHENSIVE MARKETING PLAN EXAMPLE
- PRINT MARKETING EXAMPLES
- BRANDED COMPANY MATERIALS
- DEFINE YOUR PROCESS

03.

MODULE 1 | SECTION 3

MARKETING
SECTION 3
Introduction

Brand Marketing

Marketing services play a crucial role in the success and growth of real estate professionals or companies, serving as the *foundation* upon which businesses attract clients, promote listings, and establish brand awareness in the market. In the competitive real estate industry, having a strong marketing strategy is essential for standing out from the competition and reaching target audiences effectively. There is a wide range of companies offering various marketing services tailored to the specific needs of real estate professionals, including digital marketing agencies, branding experts, and advertising firms. These services can help streamline promotional efforts, enhance visibility, and drive engagement with potential clients.

Build Your Personal Brand

Branding is not only one of the most critical components of a real estate business but also the most diverse, as it *influences* every aspect of how a business interacts with clients and stakeholders. From the design of marketing materials to the tone of communications and the overall customer experience, branding plays a central role in shaping the reputation and success of a real estate company or business. By investing in effective marketing and branding strategies, real estate professionals can differentiate themselves in the market, establish a strong presence, and build lasting relationships with clients based on trust and credibility.

Be Consistent

Consistent marketing and branding efforts are key to simplifying and establishing a real estate business, team, or firm in the market. By maintaining a *consistent brand identity* and messaging across all marketing channels, businesses can create a cohesive and recognizable presence that resonates with their target audience. Branding is not just about creating a logo or color scheme; it encompasses the values, personality, and unique selling points of the business. It is the face of how a real estate business, team, or firm communicates and delivers services to its clients, shaping perceptions and building trust.

BUILD YOUR COMPREHENSIVE MARKETING PLAN

Identify Your Needs:
Review your marketing plan and determine what specific resources, vendors, or services you will need to execute each aspect of the plan effectively. This could include professional photography, videography, social media management, website development, graphic design, and more. Using professional property marketing vendors is key to maximizing your marketing efforts.

Research and Vet Potential Partners:
Take the time to research and vet potential vendors, content creators, and service providers to ensure they align with your goals, budget, and brand values. Look for testimonials, reviews, and examples of their work to gauge their expertise and reliability.

Establish Partnerships:
Once you have identified suitable partners, reach out to them to discuss your marketing plan, goals, and expectations. Establish clear communication channels, timelines, and deliverables to ensure a smooth collaboration.

Set Expectations and Timelines:
Clearly communicate your expectations, timelines, and budget constraints to your partners to avoid any misunderstandings or delays in the implementation of your marketing plan.

Monitor and Evaluate Performance:
Regularly monitor the performance of your marketing initiatives and assess the impact of the resources and services you have sourced. Make adjustments as needed to optimize your strategies and achieve your desired outcomes.

By collaborating with these *essential contacts*, real estate agents can effectively market properties, attract potential buyers, and ultimately facilitate successful transactions. Each of these resources plays a key role in presenting properties in the best possible light and providing buyers with visuals and valuable information.

MARKETING YOUR LISTINGS

Company Colors:

Colors are important in creating a brand identity for your real estate business as they can convey emotions, set the tone for your brand, and make your brand easily recognizable to potential clients.

Company Fonts:

Company name, fonts, sizing, and requirements are crucial in establishing a professional and cohesive brand image for your real estate business. Consistency in these elements helps build trust and recognition among clients.

Company Logo:

A well-designed company logo is essential for creating a strong visual identity for your real estate business. It should be memorable, versatile, and reflect the values and services of your company.

Company Logo Variations:

Having variations of your company logo, such as horizontal and vertical layouts, color and black-and-white options, and simplified versions, ensures that your branding remains consistent across different platforms and materials.

Slogan: [Example] "Your Universal Real Estate Coach and Consultant"

A slogan and biography can help communicate the unique selling points and values of your real estate business to potential clients. They can also help differentiate your business from competitors and create a memorable impression.

Yard Signs | For Sale Signs | Directionals | Open House Signs

Ordering a variety of signs that meet your specific business needs is crucial for establishing a strong brand presence and effectively promoting your real estate business. Different types of signs serve different purposes, whether it's for property listings, open houses, branding, or directional signage. By having a diverse range of signs, you can cater to various marketing and promotional needs, attract potential clients, and enhance visibility in the market.

It's important to ensure that all branding and signage *comply* with national, state, and local municipal regulations. Each jurisdiction may have specific requirements regarding the size, placement, design, and content of signs used for residential and commercial purposes. Adhering to these regulations not only ensures legal compliance but also maintains a professional image and avoids potential fines or penalties. Branding consistency across all signage is also essential for reinforcing brand recognition and establishing a cohesive brand identity. Using consistent colors, logos, fonts, and messaging on all signage helps build brand awareness, instills trust in clients, and sets your business apart from competitors.

In the realm of marketing and real estate, there are two distinct types of marketing approaches that play crucial roles in driving success and growth in the industry. *Firm/ business to-agent marketing and agent-to-client marketing.* Below are some explanations of how you may differentiate between firm/business-to-agent marketing and agent-to- client marketing, each serving different purposes and targeting distinct audiences. As an independent agent you will essentially be responsible for all business and client marketing. Here are the key differences between the two:

1. FIRM | Business to Agent Marketing:

firm/business-to-agent marketing involves strategies and initiatives implemented by a real estate business to promote its services, brand, and value proposition to its agents or teams. This type of marketing focuses on attracting and retaining top talent, fostering a positive company culture, and providing resources and support to agents to help them succeed in their roles. Firm/business-to-agent marketing may include training programs, mentorship opportunities, lead generation tools, branding materials, and other resources aimed at empowering agents and enhancing their performance within the firm/business.

2. PUBLIC | Agent to Client Marketing:

Agent-to-client marketing, on the other hand, refers to the efforts made by individual agents or teams to attract, engage, and retain clients in the real estate market. This type of marketing focuses on building personal brand awareness, establishing credibility, and nurturing relationships with potential and existing clients. Agent-to-client marketing strategies may include social media campaigns, email newsletters, networking events, property listings, virtual tours, and personalized communication to showcase properties, provide market insights, and offer exceptional customer service to clients.

While firm/business-to-agent marketing aims to *support and empower* agents within the organization, agent-to-client marketing is geared towards *connecting with clients*, addressing their needs, and ultimately driving business growth and success. Both types of marketing are essential in the real estate industry, as they work in tandem to create a strong and reputable brand presence, attract clients, and foster long-term relationships that lead to sustainable business growth and profitability. By understanding the differences between firm/business-to-agent and agent-to-client marketing, real estate professionals can develop comprehensive marketing strategies that cater to the needs of both their internal team members and external clients, ultimately positioning themselves for success in a competitive market.

Lockboxes:

Lockboxes are used to securely store keys to a property and provide access to authorized individuals, such as agents and potential buyers. The responsibility for providing and managing lockboxes may vary depending on the brokerage or agency's policies. Some brokerages may provide lockbox services as part of their offerings, while others may require agents to purchase or rent lockboxes independently.

Signs:

Real estate signs, such as yard signs and directional signs, are essential for marketing properties and attracting potential buyers. The responsibility for ordering, installing, and maintaining signs may depend on the brokerage's policies or individual agent agreements. Some brokerages may provide branded signs for their agents, while others may require agents to procure their own signage.

Business Cards:

Business cards are a fundamental marketing tool for real estate agents to promote their services, provide contact information, and make a professional impression on clients and prospects. Agents are typically responsible for designing and ordering their own business cards, although some brokerages may offer branded business card templates, digital business cards, or assistance with printing.

Agent Branded Digital Marketing Materials:

Agent-branded digital marketing materials, such as social media graphics, email campaigns, and digital advertisements, help agents promote their services online and attract leads. Agents are usually responsible for creating or commissioning their own branded digital marketing materials, although some brokerages may provide marketing support or resources for agents.

Client Branded Digital Marketing Materials:

Client-branded digital marketing materials, such as property listings, virtual tours, and personalized communications, are designed to showcase properties and engage potential buyers or sellers. The responsibility for creating and distributing client-branded digital marketing materials typically falls on the agent, who works closely with clients to tailor the materials to their needs and preferences. Each company will operate differently.

Standardizing processes in company operations, presentations, print marketing, just listed marketing, print mail shipping, and the display of marketing materials is crucial for maintaining consistency, efficiency, and quality in real estate business practices. By establishing standardized procedures and guidelines, real estate agents can enhance their brand image, improve communication with clients, and streamline marketing efforts to drive success in the industry.

Presentations:
Standardizing presentation templates, content, and delivery methods ensures that agents present a consistent and polished image to clients. Having standardized presentation materials can help agents effectively communicate key information, showcase properties, and highlight their expertise.

Print Marketing:
Standardizing print marketing materials, such as brochures, flyers, and postcards, ensures a consistent look and messaging across all printed materials. This helps maintain brand consistency and professionalism in marketing efforts.

Just Listed Marketing:
Standardizing the process for promoting new listings helps ensure that all properties receive the same level of exposure and marketing efforts. Consistent messaging and branding in just listed marketing materials can attract potential buyers and generate interest in the property.

Print Mail Shipping:
Standardizing the process for printing and shipping marketing materials, such as postcards or newsletters, helps streamline operations and ensure timely delivery to clients. Consistency in the printing and shipping process can help agents manage costs and maintain quality control.

Display of Marketing Materials:
Standardizing how marketing materials are displayed, whether in physical offices or online platforms, can enhance the visibility and impact of the materials. Consistent display of marketing materials helps create a cohesive brand image and reinforces the professionalism of the business.

NOTE: The following step-by-step marketing plan is an example of an *effective and efficient* strategy for marketing a luxury listing. Real estate professionals are encouraged to customize and tailor their own marketing plans based on their unique services, partnerships, and target audience to maximize results and success in selling properties. By utilizing a combination of traditional and digital marketing tactics, networking opportunities, and strategic partnerships, real estate agents can effectively promote and sell listings while providing exceptional value and service to all of their clients. It is important to hire a professional to complete the following marketing tasks. Professional vendors have the skills, knowledge, and vision to create aesthetically pleasing and effective marketing materials consistently.

Staging: Hire a professional stager to enhance the visual appeal of the property and create a welcoming atmosphere for potential buyers.

Photography: Hire a professional photographer to capture high-quality images of the property, highlighting its key features and selling points.

Video: Create a video tour of the property to give potential buyers a virtual walkthrough experience and showcase the property's interior and exterior.

Lifestyle Video: Produce a lifestyle video that highlights the surrounding neighborhood, amenities, and attractions to give buyers a sense of the lifestyle offered by the property.

Drone / Arial: Utilize drone photography or aerial video to capture stunning aerial views of the property and its surroundings, providing a unique perspective for buyers.

Matter-port / Virtual Tours: Create a 3D virtual tour of the property using Matter-port technology, allowing buyers to explore the space from anywhere at any time.

Public Marketing Ad: Advertise the listing on popular real estate websites, social media platforms, and online listing portals to reach a wider audience of potential buyers.

Just Listed Postcards: Send out just listed postcards to targeted neighborhoods and potential buyers to announce the availability of the property and generate interest.

Neighborhood Letter: Send out a neighborhood letter introducing the property to nearby residents and inviting them to share the listing with friends and family who may be interested.

Property Brochure/ Flyers: Design and print professional property brochures and flyers to distribute at open houses, showings, and local businesses to provide detailed information about the property.

Open House: Host an open house event to showcase the property to potential buyers, real estate agents, and the local community.

Broker Open: Host a broker open house to give real estate agents an exclusive preview of the property and encourage collaboration and networking within the industry.

Door Hangers: Distribute door hangers in the neighborhood to promote the open house event and invite residents to visit the property.

Marketing Book: Create a comprehensive marketing book or digital portfolio that includes all marketing materials, property details, and highlights to present to potential buyers and agents.

Social Posts: Share photos, videos, and property information on social media platforms to reach a wider audience and engage with potential buyers online.

Signs/ Directionals: Install property signs in high-traffic areas to attract the attention of passersby and neighborhood traffic to the listing.

Install Lockbox: Install a lockbox on the property to provide secure access for real estate agents and potential buyers to view the property.

Display Marketing Materials: Ensure that all marketing materials, such as brochures, flyers, and property information sheets, are prominently displayed at open houses and showings for easy access by interested buyers.

Property Information Sheets: Create detailed property information sheets that highlight the key features, amenities, and selling points of the property to provide to potential buyers.

Listing Agent Information: Include contact information for the listing agent on all marketing materials and property listings to make it easy for interested buyers to reach out with questions or to schedule a showing.

It is important to note that the marketing and level of marketing may vary from firm to firm or property to property. However, streamlining your marketing process can help create the same level of standards and expectations, building brand consistency regardless of the price point of the property. By establishing a set of guidelines, templates, and strategies for marketing properties, you can ensure that each listing receives the same level of attention and promotion, maintaining brand consistency and professionalism across all your marketing efforts.

PRINT MARKETING

Source a local printer for efficiency

Here is a list of print materials commonly used in real estate marketing:

Business Partner Guide: A professionally designed book containing information about the business, team, or firm, and the services offered to both clients and agents.

1. Listing Presentations: A comprehensive package that showcases a property for sale, including details about the property, market analysis, and the agent's marketing plan.

2. Buyer Presentations: A presentation tailored to potential buyers, highlighting the agent's services, the buying process, and available properties.

3. Listing - Public Presentation Book: A professionally designed book containing information about the agent, business, team, or firm, the listing details, and any additional features, floor plans, or upgrades.

4. Farming Postcards: Postcards sent to a specific geographic area to generate leads and build brand awareness.

5. Just Listed Postcards: Postcards announcing a new listing to potential buyers in the area.

6. Flyers: One-page marketing materials that provide information about a property or the agent's services.

7. Brochures: Multi-page marketing materials that offer a more detailed overview of a property or the agent's services.

8. Door Hangers: Marketing materials hung on the doorknobs of potential clients' homes to promote listings, open houses, or services.

9. Client Letters: Personalized letters sent to clients to provide updates, market information, or other relevant content.

10. Newsletters: Regularly distributed publications containing valuable information, market updates, real estate tips, and information about the agent's listings and services.

When presenting options to clients, it is important to showcase the value of professionally designed print materials in marketing their property effectively. Highlight the impact of high-quality visuals and well-crafted messaging on attracting buyers and generating interest in their listing.

To maximize the impact of branded company materials, it is essential to make these options available to employees, clients, and other stakeholders. By offering a variety of branded merchandise and promotional items, you can create additional revenue streams, increase brand visibility, and strengthen brand loyalty among customers and employees. Standardizing the design, quality, and distribution of branded company materials is crucial to maintaining consistency and coherence in your brand messaging. By establishing clear brand guidelines and ensuring that all materials adhere to these standards, you can reinforce brand recognition, build trust with your audience, and create a unified brand experience.

Bags, Backpacks, Totes:
- These branded items are not only practical but also serve as a stylish and functional way for agents to carry their essentials.

Branded Presentation Binders:
- Presentation binders customized with your company logo and branding can elevate the professionalism of your agents' presentations.

Sample Templates | Presentation Materials:
- Offering sample presentation materials or templates, such as brochures, flyers, and promotional items, can be a valuable resource for agents to showcase properties and market their services effectively.

Clothing (T-Shirts, Sweatshirts, and Jackets):
- Branded clothing items like T-shirts, sweatshirts, and jackets featuring your company logo can create a sense of unity and cohesiveness among your team members.

Tumblers, Coffee Cups, Wine Glasses:
- Personalized drink-ware items like tumblers, coffee cups, and wine glasses make for practical and thoughtful gifts for agents and partners.

MARKETING

MODULE 1 | SECTION 3
Conclusion

Once you have determined whether you will utilize an in-house marketing department or partner with external services for your marketing needs, it is essential to establish standards on how you, your team, or business will deliver marketing materials to both agents and clients. By *setting clear guidelines and expectations* for the creation and distribution of marketing materials, you can ensure consistency, professionalism, and alignment with your brand identity and messaging.

Whether you choose to have an in-house marketing team or work with external partners, it is crucial to define the connection points through which marketing materials will be shared with agents and clients. This includes establishing communication channels, timelines, approval processes, and feedback mechanisms to facilitate a smooth and efficient workflow. Agents should be made aware of these connection points and trained on how to effectively utilize them to access and leverage marketing materials for their listings and client interactions.

By setting clear connection points, providing training and support, and enforcing standards for marketing materials delivery, you can optimize your marketing efforts, empower your team, and create a seamless and professional experience for agents and clients alike. This strategic approach will help you maximize the impact of your marketing initiatives and strengthen your brand presence in the competitive real estate market.

MARKETING
MODULE 1 | SECTION 3
Conclusion

MANAGE YOUR MARKETING...

Choose the print materials you will offer in your marketing plan, add the printing company you will partner with for materials, or the preferred vendor for ordering print materials. Partnering with a local printer can greatly reduce the time for delivery of materials.

By setting connection points to partners or platforms and ensuring that agents are well-informed about how to utilize them, you can streamline the marketing process, enhance collaboration, and empower agents to effectively promote their listings and engage with clients. Consistent communication and training on the use of marketing materials and resources will help agents leverage these tools to attract leads, showcase properties, and deliver exceptional service to their clients. Additionally, by establishing standards for the delivery of marketing materials, you can maintain brand consistency, drive engagement, and build credibility with both agents and clients.

ASK YOURSELF...

Once you have created your personalized marketing plan for your Individual real estate business, team, or firm, it is important to source the necessary resources, vendors, content creators, and any other services needed to power the plan effectively. These resources and partners will play a crucial role in implementing your marketing strategies and reaching your target audience successfully, and consistently.

- What contacts or connections will you need to power your marketing plan?
- Who will design your content?
- Who will be responsible for each piece of your plan?
- Where will you store company materials or templates?
- Who will print your marketing materials?
- Do you have a local printing partner?
- What will you do differently to set you apart when marketing properties?
- Have you documented the details of your plan?
- Have you defined your property marketing standards?

LAW OF CORRESPONDENCE:

THE PATTERNS AND STRATEGIES YOU ESTABLISH IN YOUR BUSINESS REFLECT BROADER PRINCIPLES OF SUCCESS. BY IDENTIFYING AND REPLICATING EFFECTIVE STRATEGIES, SUCH AS TARGETED MARKETING OR EXCEPTIONAL CLIENT SERVICE, YOU CAN ACHIEVE CONSISTENT RESULTS. THIS LAW EMPHASIZES THE IMPORTANCE OF LEARNING FROM SUCCESSFUL PRACTICES AND APPLYING THEM TO ENHANCE CLIENT SATISFACTION AND BUSINESS OUTCOMES.

BUSINESS OPERATIONS MANUAL

DOCUMENTS | COORDINATION

- DOCUMENTS - COORDINATION INTRODUCTION DETAILS
- SOME TASKS A DOCUMENT SUPPORT PERSON MAY PERFORM
- SELECT YOUR DOCUMENT SUPPORT STRUCTURE

04.

MODULE 1 | SECTION 4

DOCUMENTS | COORDINATION

SECTION 4
Introduction

By setting up transaction coordination services effectively and clearly defining the processes, expectations, and costs associated with this function, real estate business owners, operators and agents can streamline their operations, enhance client experiences, and drive business growth. *Leveraging technology and professional support* in transaction coordination can help real estate professionals optimize their operations, improve efficiency, and deliver exceptional service to clients, customers, and partners in the dynamic world of real estate today.

When starting out as a real estate agent, managing the myriad of tasks involved in each transaction can be overwhelming. This is where the advice to utilize a pay-by-service transaction coordinator comes into play. By opting for this flexible support model, new agents can gain immediate assistance in managing their transactions without the financial burden of hiring a full-time coordinator. This approach allows agents to focus on building their client base and honing their sales skills while ensuring that the administrative aspects of their business are handled efficiently.

Using a pay-by-service transaction coordinator provides several advantages. First and foremost, it offers agents the flexibility to scale their support based on their current workload. As a new agent, you may have fluctuating transaction volumes, and paying for services only when needed helps control expenses. This model allows agents to allocate their resources more effectively, avoiding the fixed costs associated with a full-time hire, which can be particularly crucial during the initial stages of their careers when cash flow may be limited.

Additionally, having access to a transaction coordinator from day one can significantly enhance the professionalism and efficiency of an agent's operations. These coordinators are experienced in managing the paperwork and compliance requirements that come with real estate transactions, ensuring that nothing falls through the cracks. This support not only streamlines processes but also allows agents to provide a higher level of service to their clients, fostering trust and satisfaction. Ultimately, leveraging a pay-by-service transaction coordinator can be a strategic move for new real estate agents, enabling them to kickstart their careers with the right balance of support and financial prudence.

A transaction coordinator plays an important role in managing the complex process of buying or selling a property, ensuring compliance with legal requirements, and facilitating communication between all parties involved in the transaction. Make a note that each coordinators services and prices will vary. Finding a transaction coordinator that is able to scale with your goals, and fulfill your vision of service can greatly impact your rate of consistency through growth. Here are some key considerations to keep in mind…

In-House Vs. Virtual Assistance:
Determine whether your business, team, or firm will have an in-house transaction coordinator, utilize virtual assistance, or require agents to handle their own transaction documents. Each option has its own set of advantages and considerations, such as cost, efficiency, and scalability.

Level of Service:
Clarify the scope of transaction coordination services that will be offered, including tasks such as document management, contract review, deadline tracking, and communication with clients and other parties. Define the level of service that coordinators will provide to ensure consistency and quality throughout the transaction process.

Fees and Costs:
Determine if there will be any fees or costs associated with transaction coordination services. This may include flat fees, commission splits, or other compensation structures for the coordinators. Clearly communicate these terms to agents and clients to avoid any misunderstandings or disputes.

Points of Connection:
Establish clear points of connection and communication channels for how transaction coordination services will operate within your business, team, or firm. Define roles, responsibilities, and expectations for all parties involved to ensure a smooth and efficient transaction process.

DISCLAIMER:
It is recommended to consult with legal counsel or regulatory authorities to ensure adherence to all local, state, and national applicable laws and regulations when using a transaction coordinator. It is always advised to seek a licensed TC, even when it is not required.

Preparing a Listing Presentation: A transaction coordinator may assist in preparing a comprehensive listing presentation for a property, including gathering property information, creating marketing materials, and showcasing the property's features and highlights to attract potential sellers.

Preparing Property Information | MLS Entry: The transaction coordinator can gather all relevant property information, such as square footage, amenities, and photos, and enter this data into the Multiple Listing Service (MLS) to make the property visible to agents and potential buyers.

Prepare CMA: Comparative Market Analysis - Not all transaction coordinators perform this task: Sourcing a local TC can be beneficial.

Writing an Offer to Purchase: The transaction coordinator can assist in drafting an offer to purchase document, outlining the terms and conditions of the buyer's offer to purchase the property. This includes details such as the purchase price, contingencies, and closing timeline.

Managing Essential Documents: The transaction coordinator is responsible for managing and organizing all essential documents related to the transaction, including contracts, addendums, disclosures, and other paperwork required for the sale or purchase of the property.

Managing Essential Property Vendors: The transaction coordinator may coordinate with essential property vendors, such as inspectors, appraisers, title companies, and lenders, to ensure that all necessary services are scheduled and completed in a timely manner.

Submitting Closing Documents for Compliance: The transaction coordinator is responsible for submitting all closing documents to ensure compliance with legal and regulatory requirements. This includes coordinating with all parties involved in the transaction to gather and organize the necessary paperwork for a successful closing.

Every real estate firm, team, or individual operates differently, and the transaction coordination and compliance services available will vary from one firm, team, or individual to another. Some companies may have *in-house* transaction coordinators and compliance specialists, while others may rely on *external* providers or agents to handle these tasks. By utilizing a transaction coordinator for some or all of your services, you can add leverage and greatly enhance your operations in several ways.

Expertise: Transaction coordinators are trained professionals who specialize in managing real estate transactions from start to finish. They have a thorough understanding of the legal requirements, documentation, and timelines involved in a real estate transaction, ensuring that all aspects are handled efficiently and accurately.

Time Saving: Outsourcing transaction coordination and compliance services to a dedicated coordinator frees up your time as a real estate agent to focus on building client relationships, generating leads, and closing deals. This allows you to be more productive and efficient in your day-to-day operations.

Compliance: Real estate transactions involve complex legal and regulatory requirements that must be met to ensure a smooth and successful closing. Transaction coordinators are well-versed in these requirements and can help ensure that all documentation is accurate, complete, and in compliance with relevant laws and regulations.

Enhanced Operations: You can streamline your operations, reduce errors and delays, and improve the overall efficiency of your real estate business by leveraging the expertise of a transaction coordinator. This can lead to increased productivity, client satisfaction, and profitability.

Compliance Only Transaction Coordinators: Some transaction coordinators specialize in compliance-related tasks, ensuring that all documents and processes adhere to industry regulations and standards. These coordinators focus on maintaining accurate records, verifying information, and ensuring that the transaction progresses smoothly without any compliance issues.

It is important to note that transaction coordination services may vary based on local regulations and business, team, or firm policies. While the above list includes potential services, partners, vendors, and connections that can power a real estate business, it is essential to verify which services are available and ensure compliance with all legal requirements. Agents and brokers may still be held responsible for any omissions or errors on their behalf, regardless of the services or tasks completed by the coordinator.

DOCUMENTS | COORDINATION
MODULE 1 | SECTION 4
Conclusion

MANAGE YOUR DOCUMENTS...

Document support staff plays a crucial role in managing the complex process of buying or selling a property, ensuring compliance with legal requirements, and facilitating communication between all parties involved in the transaction. Work through the list of the document support services that you may need or want to add, and add any additional options that may fit your model. You will need to compile the details.

ASK YOURSELF...

- Will you use a transaction coordinator?
- Who will manage compliance?
- What level of service do you desire?
- What services will you use a support person for?
- If you have agents affiliated with your team or firm, what will each be responsible for?
- Will you have in house or virtual Transaction assistance?

BUSINESS OPERATIONS MANUAL

CUSTOMER RELATIONSHIP MANAGEMENT [CRM]

- CRM INTRODUCTION | CHOOSING YOUR CRM
- CRM CONNECTIONS AND INTEGRATION
- CRM PROCESS AND PROCEDURES
- CONSISTENT AND STRATEGIC USE OF YOUR CRM SYSTEM

05.

MODULE 1 | SECTION 5

CUSTOMER RELATIONSHIP MANAGEMENT

SECTION 5
Introduction

Real estate professionals should consider their specific goals, needs, and budget to select a solution that *aligns* with their business objectives. There are various types of CRM (Customer Relationship Management) systems available, ranging from basic contact management tools to advanced platforms with robust features, customization options, and integration capabilities. Agents should *evaluate factors* such as user-friendliness, scalability, mobile accessibility, customer support, and pricing when selecting a CRM system that best suits their individual or team requirements. After selecting a system to manage your relationships, you will need to set up your systems, and develop your unique usage process.

Choosing the right Customer Relationship Management system is a crucial decision for independent real estate agents, teams, or firms as it can significantly impact their business growth and success. A CRM system serves as a centralized platform for managing client relationships, leads, transactions, communications, and marketing efforts. It helps real estate professionals streamline their operations, enhance client interactions, and drive business growth by providing valuable insights, automation capabilities, and organizational tools.

By setting clear standards and processes for using the CRM system, real estate professionals can streamline their operations, enhance client relationships, and drive business growth effectively. Consistent data management, personalized communication, and targeted marketing efforts will help agents stay top of mind with clients and prospects, ultimately leading to increased engagement and success in the competitive real estate market.

YOUR CRM SYSTEM

Efficient Client Management:
A CRM system allows agents to store and organize client information, preferences, and communication history in one place, making it easier to track interactions, follow up on leads, and provide personalized services to clients.

Lead Generation | Conversion:
CRM systems help agents capture, nurture, and convert leads by automating lead management processes, tracking lead sources, and sending targeted marketing campaigns to engage potential clients effectively.

Task | Transaction Management:
Real estate transactions involve numerous tasks, deadlines, and documents that need to be managed efficiently. A CRM system can help agents stay organized, track transaction progress, set reminders, and collaborate with clients and team members seamlessly.

Marketing | Communication:
CRM systems offer tools for creating and sending email campaigns, newsletters, and personalized communications to clients, helping agents stay top of mind, nurture relationships, and promote listings effectively.

Reporting | Analytics:
CRM systems provide valuable insights into client behavior, lead sources, marketing performance, and sales metrics, enabling agents to make data-driven decisions, identify trends, and optimize their strategies for better results.

Once a CRM system been chosen, it is important to establish standards and processes for adding prospects or clients to the system, defining criteria for listing them, creating touch points, determining user interactions, managing documents, and creating campaigns and communications. Here are some considerations for each aspect:

Adding Prospects | Clients: Define a clear process for adding new prospects or clients to the CRM system, ensuring that all relevant information is captured accurately. Establish protocols for updating and maintaining client records in the CRM system to ensure data integrity.

Criteria | Listing Prospects or Clients: Determine specific criteria for categorizing prospects or clients within the CRM system, such as lead status, property preferences, communication history, or transaction stage. Segment clients based on their needs, preferences, and engagement level to personalize interactions and marketing efforts effectively.

Touch Points: Develop a series of touch points or communication strategies to engage with prospects and clients at various stages of the real estate process, such as initial contact, property search, offer negotiation, and closing. Implement automated reminders or follow-up sequences to stay in touch with clients and provide timely updates.

User Interactions: Define when and how users, such as agents or team members, should interact with the CRM system, including data entry, updating client information, scheduling tasks, and tracking communication. Provide training and resources to ensure that users understand how to leverage the CRM system effectively for their workflows.

Document Management: Establish protocols for managing documents within the CRM system, including uploading, organizing, and sharing files related to transactions, contracts, disclosures, and client communications. Implement version control and access permissions to ensure that documents are secure and accessible to authorized users.

Creating Campaigns | Personalized Communications: Determine whether agents will be responsible for creating campaigns, newsletters, and personalized communications within the CRM system or if the firm will provide templates or content. Develop a content strategy and calendar for delivering relevant and engaging communications to clients, such as market updates, property listings, industry insights, and promotional offers.

Company Compliant Templates: Create compliant templates within your company's chosen platform for standardizing documents and agreements. Customize templates to reflect your branding, legal requirements, and specific transaction needs. Ensure that templates adhere to industry regulations and best practices for consistency and accuracy.

Compliance Procedures: Implement compliance procedures within your CRM or compliance system to ensure regulatory adherence. Define compliance checkpoints, document verification processes, and audit trails for transparency and accountability. Regularly review and update compliance protocols to align with industry changes and legal requirements.

Smart Plan Creation: Build smart plans within your chosen system to automate tasks, reminders, and follow-ups throughout the transaction life cycle. Customize smart plans based on transaction types, client preferences, and company workflows. Monitor smart plans for effectiveness and make adjustments as needed to optimize efficiency.

Campaign Management: Create campaigns within your chosen system to market listings, promote services, and engage with clients. Design targeted campaigns based on client segmentation, demographics, and preferences. Track campaign performance metrics to evaluate effectiveness and make data-driven decisions.

Technology Usage Guidelines: Provide agents with a comprehensive guide on how to use technology within the company, including CRM systems, signature platforms, compliance tools, and marketing software. Offer training sessions, tutorials, and resources to help agents navigate technology tools effectively. Encourage agents to explore different technology options and choose tools that align with their workflow and business objectives.

Consistent data management, personalized communication, and targeted marketing efforts will help agents stay top of mind with clients and prospects, ultimately leading to increased engagement, connections, and relationships.

When starting a new business or embarking on a career as a real estate agent, integrating technology into your operations is crucial for efficiency and success. Here is a breakdown of some key components and considerations when leveraging compliance technology in your real estate business. Make notes of specific company platform connections, protocols, integrations, and attach company training videos for any of the necessary steps for agents, and staff new to the team, firm, or real estate business.

1.Signature Platform: A signature platform is essential for electronically signing documents, contracts, and agreements. It streamlines the process of obtaining signatures, reduces paperwork, and accelerates transaction timelines. Selecting a reliable and user-friendly signature platform is crucial for ensuring seamless document management.

2.CRM or Compliance System Integration with Signature Platform: Integrating your CRM (Customer Relationship Management) system with your signature platform enhances workflow efficiency. This integration allows for seamless transfer of client information, document tracking, and automated signature requests. Ensure that your CRM and signature platform are compatible and can communicate effectively to streamline transactions.

3.Beginning a Transaction for Compliance Submission: Utilize your CRM or compliance system to initiate a transaction and ensure compliance with industry regulations. Input relevant client and property information, upload necessary documents, and track key milestones throughout the transaction process. Compliance submission within your CRM helps maintain accurate records and ensures adherence to legal requirements.

4.Company Document Management: Store specific company documents in a centralized location within your chosen platform or document management system. Access company documents securely by setting up user permissions and authentication protocols. Organize documents into folders or categories for easy retrieval and reference.

5.Document Transfer Between Platforms: Transfer documents between platforms by exporting files from one system and importing them into another. Use compatible file formats for seamless transfer and ensure data integrity during the process. Maintain document version control to avoid discrepancies and errors.

CRM systems offer a centralized platform for managing customer interactions, sales, marketing, and more, providing numerous benefits for real estate operations. By utilizing a CRM system effectively, real estate professionals can enhance customer service by maintaining detailed client profiles, tracking interactions, and personalizing communication.

Lead Management: Use your CRM system to track and manage leads efficiently, ensuring timely follow-ups and personalized communication with potential clients.

Property Management: Keep detailed records of all properties in your CRM system, including property details, photos, and status updates.

Client Communication: Utilize CRM tools to send automated emails, newsletters, and updates to clients, keeping them informed about new listings and market trends.

Task Management: Create tasks and reminders within your CRM system to stay organized and on top of important deadlines, appointments, and follow-ups.

Document Storage: Store important documents, contracts, and agreements in your CRM system for easy access and retrieval.

Reporting and Analytics: Generate reports and analyze data within your CRM system to track performance, monitor trends, and make informed business decisions.

Referral Tracking: Keep track of referrals and recommendations from clients within your CRM system to reward loyal customers and incentivize referrals.

Open House Management: Use your CRM system to manage and track open house events, including attendee lists, feedback, and follow-up actions.

Marketing Campaigns: Create and manage marketing campaigns within your CRM system, including email campaigns, social media ads, and targeted promotions.

Client Segmentation: Segment your client database in your CRM system based on criteria such as location, budget, and preferences to tailor your communication and marketing efforts. Managing invitations, registrations, and follow-ups.

Integration with Listing Platforms: Integrate your CRM system with listing platforms to automatically update property listings and synchronize data across platforms.

Mobile Access: Utilize mobile CRM apps to access important information, communicate with clients, and manage tasks while on the go.

Automated Workflows: Set up automated workflows in your CRM system to streamline processes, save time, and ensure consistency in client interactions.

Social Media Management: Monitor and engage with clients on social media platforms through your CRM system, tracking interactions and building relationships.

Client Feedback: Collect and analyze client feedback within your CRM system to identify areas for improvement and enhance customer satisfaction.

Vendor Management: Manage relationships with vendors, contractors, and service providers within your CRM system, keeping track of services, costs, and performance.

Training and Development: Use your CRM system to provide training materials, resources, and updates to agents, ensuring they are informed and equipped to succeed.

Event Planning: Plan and organize real estate events, seminars, and workshops within your CRM system, managing invitations, registrations, and follow-ups.

Property Valuation: Utilize CRM tools to track property valuations, market trends, and appraisal information, helping clients make informed decisions.

Customer Loyalty Programs: Implement customer loyalty programs within your CRM system to reward repeat clients, encourage referrals, and foster long-term relationships.

CUSTOMER RELATIONSHIP MANAGEMENT
MODULE 1 | SECTION 5
Conclusion

MANAGE YOUR RELATIONSHIPS...

CRM systems can streamline operations by automating tasks, managing leads efficiently, and providing valuable insights through data analytics. Consistent and strategic use of a CRM system can lead to improved efficiency, better decision-making, and ultimately, enhanced customer satisfaction. Work through the comprehensive list of connections, processes, and procedures. Once you have selected the CRM system you will use, you will need to make detailed notes about your company's protocols, connections, or integrations with other platforms if available.

ASK YOURSELF...

- Have you created a plan for consistent and strategic use of your CRM system?
- Have you documented the process and procedures for using your CRM system?
- Have you created instructions for any company CRM integrations?
- Who will be responsible for using, maintaining, and updating the CRM system?
- Will your CRM be connected to a lead source? Do you have a follow up plan for company leads?
- Where and how will you store company CRM plans, workflows, and company processes?

UNIVERSAL LAW OF COMPENSATION:

THE SERVICE LEVEL YOU PROVIDE DIRECTLY IMPACTS THE REWARDS YOU RECEIVE. IN REAL ESTATE, GOING ABOVE AND BEYOND FOR CLIENTS—WHETHER THROUGH PERSONALIZED SERVICE OR EXPERT ADVICE—ENHANCES YOUR REPUTATION AND INCREASES FINANCIAL GAIN POTENTIAL. THIS LAW UNDERSCORES THE VALUE OF INVESTING IN CLIENT RELATIONSHIPS AND DELIVERING EXCEPTIONAL SERVICE TO ACHIEVE BUSINESS SUCCESS.

BUSINESS OPERATIONS MANUAL

TECHNOLOGY AND SOCIAL MEDIA

- TECHNOLOGY AND SOCIAL MEDIA INTRODUCTION
- SOCIAL MEDIA BENEFITS | TERMS
- MARKETING VIDEOS
- DIGITAL DESIGN | QUICK CONTENT
- SOCIAL MEDIA MARKETING
- ARTIFICIAL INTELLIGENCE
- REAL ESTATE CHATBOT
- USING AI THE NEW ASSISTANT
- USING ARTIFICIAL INTELLIGENCE
- CREATING A PERSONALIZED CHATBOT
- TECHNOLOGY
- HYPERLINK ENHANCEMENT

06.

MODULE 1 | SECTION 6

TECHNOLOGY AND SOCIAL MEDIA

SECTION 6
Introduction

Agents can leverage social media to stay updated on market trends, share industry insights, and connect with potential clients, ultimately enhancing their *visibility and reputation* in the market. Overall, social media has become an indispensable tool for real estate agents, empowering them to adapt to changing consumer behaviors, differentiate themselves in a competitive market, and drive business growth.

Over the last decade, social media has transformed the way real estate agents do business, revolutionizing the industry and reshaping how agents connect with clients, market properties, and build their brand. Social media platforms have provided real estate agents with powerful tools to reach a broader audience, engage with potential buyers and sellers, and showcase properties in innovative ways.

One of the key ways social media has changed the real estate industry is by offering agents a *cost-effective and efficient* way to market and generate leads. Agents can create targeted ads, share virtual tours, and engage with clients in real-time, creating a more personalized and interactive experience for buyers and sellers. Social media has also allowed agents to build their online presence, establish credibility, and showcase their expertise through content marketing, blogging, and video marketing. Social media has facilitated networking and relationship-building opportunities for real estate agents, enabling them to connect with industry professionals, collaborate with partners, and *expand their sphere* of influence.

In today's world of social media and marketing, getting comfortable on camera is essential for effectively engaging with audiences and standing out in a crowded digital landscape. Video content has become increasingly popular on social media platforms due to its ability to capture attention, convey messages more effectively, and create more connection with viewers.

CONSIDER THE FOLLOWING TIPS:

Define Your Objective: Clearly outline the purpose of the video and what you want to achieve with it.

Know Your Audience: Tailor your content to resonate with your target audience's interests, preferences, and needs.

Keep it Concise: Capture viewers' attention quickly and deliver your message in a clear and concise manner.

Use Engaging Visuals: Incorporate eye-catching visuals, graphics, and animations to make your video visually appealing.

Be Authentic: Show your personality and be genuine in your delivery to connect with viewers on a personal level.

Include a Call to Action: Encourage viewers to take a specific action, such as liking, sharing, or commenting on the video.

Optimize for Mobile: Ensure your video is optimized for viewing on mobile devices, as a significant portion of social media users access platforms on their smartphones.

Test and Iterate: Monitor the performance of your videos, gather feedback, and make adjustments to improve future content.

By incorporating video into social media marketing strategies, businesses can showcase their products or services, share valuable information, and humanize their brand, ultimately driving engagement and building relationships with their audience.

THE BENEFITS OF SOCIAL MEDIA

Reach a Wider Audience:
Social media platforms have a vast user base, allowing agents to reach a larger audience and attract potential clients from different demographics and locations.

Build Brand Awareness:
Social media provides a platform to showcase your brand, highlight your expertise, and differentiate yourself from competitors. Consistent and engaging content can help build brand recognition and establish credibility in the industry.

Engage With Clients:
Social media platforms offer a direct line of communication with clients, allowing agents to engage in conversations, address inquiries, provide updates, and offer valuable information. Engaging with clients on social media can help build relationships, foster trust, and enhance customer satisfaction.

Showcase Properties:
Social media platforms are an excellent tool for showcasing properties through photos, videos, virtual tours, and interactive content. Agents can use these platforms to highlight listings, attract buyers, and create a visually appealing portfolio of properties.

SOCIAL MEDIA TERMS

Engagement Rate: The percentage of people who interact with a piece of content, such as liking, commenting, or sharing, out of the number of people who saw the content.

Impressions: The number of times a piece of content is displayed on a user's screen, regardless of whether it is clicked or engaged with.

Click-Through Rate (CTR): The percentage of people who click on a digital advertisement or social media post compared to the total number of people who viewed the ad or post.

Reach: The total number of unique users who see a piece of content or advertisement.

Hashtag: A word or phrase preceded by the "#" symbol used on social media platforms to categorize content and make it discoverable to users interested in that topic.

SEO (Search Engine Optimization): The process of optimizing a website or content to improve its visibility and ranking on search engine results pages.

Influencer: A person with a large following on social media who can impact the opinions and purchasing decisions of their audience.

Algorithm: A set of rules or calculations used by social media platforms to determine the order and visibility of content in users feeds.

Viral: Content that spreads rapidly and widely across social media platforms, often reaching a large audience in a short period of time.

Advancements in design programs have revolutionized the way we do marketing in the real estate industry. With the proliferation of design platforms, creating professional marketing materials such as flyers, brochures, business cards, postcards, and more has become more accessible and efficient than ever before. These *design programs* offer a wide range of templates, customization options, and user-friendly interfaces, allowing real estate professionals to create *visually appealing and engaging* materials to promote their listings and services. The emergence of programs and user-friendly website builders has further transformed the real estate marketing landscape. These tools enable agents to easily create their own websites, client portals, virtual tours, and other digital assets to enhance their online presence and connect with clients in a more interactive and personalized way. The ease of use and flexibility offered by these design programs and digital tools have empowered real estate agents to take control of their marketing efforts and differentiate themselves in a competitive market.

As the real estate industry continues to evolve, embracing these advancements in design programs will be essential for staying ahead of the curve and *maximizing the impact* of your marketing efforts. In the past, promoting a property through traditional methods like postcards required a lengthy process of creating the design, sending it to a printer, and then waiting for it to be mailed out by the post office. This process could take days or even weeks, resulting in delays in reaching potential buyers and generating interest in the listing. With the advent of social media, real estate professionals can now promote properties in real-time, drastically reducing the time, energy, and connection points needed to market a listing. Digital platforms now allow agents to showcase properties instantly to a vast audience, engage with potential buyers, and generate leads quickly and efficiently. By leveraging social media, agents can reach a broader audience, engage with clients in a more personalized manner, and drive traffic to their listings in a fraction of the time it would take with traditional marketing methods.

As technology continues to rapidly evolve within the real estate industry, agents, teams, and firms must adapt to these changes in order to succeed. Staying up-to-date with the latest tools, trends, and platforms in digital marketing, virtual tours, CRM systems, and data analytics is crucial for staying *competitive* in the market. By embracing technology and leveraging its capabilities, real estate professionals can streamline their operations, enhance their marketing efforts, and provide a more seamless and engaging experience for their clients. Adapting to the changing landscape of technology in real estate is essential for staying relevant, attracting clients, and achieving success in today's fast-paced and ever-changing market.

Technology is changing the way we do marketing and real estate by providing innovative tools and platforms to reach and engage with audiences more effectively. With the rise of virtual tours, 3D modeling, drone photography, and AI-powered chatbots, real estate professionals can offer *immersive and personalized experiences* to clients from anywhere in the world. Additionally, CRM systems, marketing automation software, and data analytics tools enable agents to streamline their operations, track leads, and make data-driven decisions to optimize their marketing efforts.

1. Utilize social media platforms to showcase listings, share market updates, and engage potential clients.

2. Create high-quality visual content including photos, videos, virtual tours, and infographics to attract and engage audiences.

3. Use social media advertising to target specific demographics, interests, and locations to reach potential buyers and sellers.

4. Engage with followers by responding to comments, messages, and inquiries promptly and professionally.

5. Collaborate with influencers or local businesses to expand your reach and build credibility in the community.

6. Host virtual events, webinars, or live QandA sessions to educate and connect with your audience.

7. Share client testimonials, success stories, and case studies to showcase your expertise and build trust with potential clients.

8. Implement email marketing campaigns to nurture leads, share valuable content, and keep in touch with past clients.

9. Utilize social media analytics and insights to track performance, measure ROI, and optimize your marketing strategies.

By leveraging social media effectively, real estate professionals can build brand awareness, generate leads, engage with clients, and ultimately grow their business in a competitive market.

Artificial intelligence (AI) offers numerous benefits for various aspects of real estate, including client communication, listing descriptions, marketing materials, generating images, and creating social media posts. Here are some of the benefits of using AI in each of these areas.

1. Client Communication: AI-powered chatbots can provide instant responses to client inquiries, schedule appointments, and provide personalized recommendations based on client preferences. This improves response times, enhances customer service, and allows agents to focus on high-touch interactions with clients.

2. Listing Descriptions: AI algorithms can analyze property data, market trends, and buyer preferences to generate compelling and accurate listing descriptions. This saves time for agents and ensures that listings are optimized for maximum visibility and appeal to potential buyers.

3. Marketing Materials: AI can help automate the creation of marketing materials such as brochures, flyers, and virtual tours by generating high-quality content and visuals based on property information. This streamlines the marketing process and ensures consistent branding across all materials.

4. Generating Images: AI-powered tools can enhance property photos, create virtual staging, and even generate realistic 3D renderings of properties bringing a buyers vision to life. This attracts more potential buyers, and helps properties stand out in a competitive market.

5. Creating Social Media Posts: AI can analyze data on audience preferences, engagement metrics, and trending topics to generate engaging and relevant social media posts. This helps real estate agents maintain an active online presence, attract followers, and drive traffic to their listings.

In the future, AI is expected to be integrated into almost every aspect of real estate, from property search and valuation to transaction management and customer service. By learning to integrate AI into their operations, real estate professionals can optimize their workflows, improve efficiency, and gain a competitive edge in the market. AI can help agents save time, reduce manual tasks, and focus on building relationships, negotiating deals, and providing personalized service to clients.

A real estate chatbot is an artificial intelligence-powered tool that is designed interact with users in a conversational manner to provide information, answer questions, and assist with various real estate-related tasks. These chatbots can be integrated into websites, social media platforms, messaging apps, and communication channels to engage with clients, prospects, and website visitors in real-time.

Property Search:

- Chatbots can help users search for properties based on their preferences, such as location, price range, size, and amenities. They can provide listings, schedule property viewings, and answer questions about available properties.

Lead Generation:

- Chatbots can capture leads by collecting contact information, qualifying leads based on predefined criteria, and scheduling meetings or consultations with real estate agents.

Customer Support:

- Chatbots can provide customer support by answering frequently asked questions, providing information about services, and assisting with common inquiries.

Marketing and Promotions:

- Chatbots can deliver personalized marketing messages, promotions, and offers to users based on their preferences and behavior.

USING AI EFFECTIVELY

Here are some tips and tricks to remember while using AI for creating content for your business:

- Clearly define your content goals and objectives before using AI to ensure that the generated content aligns with your purpose.

- Provide specific and detailed prompts to guide the AI in generating relevant and accurate content.

- Use AI tools to brainstorm ideas, generate creative content, and overcome writer's block by exploring different perspectives.

- Edit and refine content generated by AI to ensure coherence, accuracy, and consistency with your brand voice.

- Incorporate keywords and SEO strategies into the content to improve search engine visibility and reach.

- Experiment with different AI models and settings to explore the full potential of AI-generated content.

- Use AI-generated content as a starting point or inspiration for further development and refinement.

- Collaborate with AI by asking follow-up questions, providing feedback, and guiding the conversation to enhance the quality of the content.

- Stay updated on AI advancements and best practices in content creation to leverage AI tools effectively.

- Keep experimenting, learning, and adapting your approach to using AI to unlock its full potential for content creation.

Real estate chatbots are becoming more common in the industry due to their ability to provide instant responses, improve customer engagement, streamline processes, and enhance the *overall* user experience. With advancements in artificial intelligence and natural language processing technologies, chatbots are becoming more sophisticated and capable of handling complex interactions with users. Real estate professionals are increasingly adopting chatbots as a *cost-effective and efficient way* to automate routine tasks, generate leads, and provide personalized services to clients. Clearly define the purpose of your chatbot, and set specific goals for its use.

- Choose a chatbot platform that aligns with your business needs and offers the features you require.
- Personalize your chatbot's responses to make interactions more engaging and relevant to users.
- Implement a seamless handoff to a human agent when the chatbot is unable to address a user's query.
- Regularly update and optimize your chatbot's knowledge base to improve its accuracy and effectiveness.
- Use a conversational tone and natural language to make interactions with the chatbot more user-friendly.
- Provide clear instructions on how users can interact with the chatbot and access the information they need.
- Test your chatbot across different devices and platforms to ensure a consistent user experience.
- Monitor and analyze chatbot interactions to identify areas for improvement and refine your chatbot's performance.
- Integrate your chatbot with other systems and tools to streamline workflows and enhance its functionality.
- Train your chatbot to handle common inquiries and provide accurate responses to user questions.
- Implement security measures to protect user data and ensure that sensitive information is handled securely.
- Offer users the option to provide feedback on their chatbot experience to gather insights for future enhancements.
- Continuously iterate and evolve your chatbot based on user feedback and performance metrics to enhance its capabilities.
- Stay informed about advancements in AI technology and chatbot development to leverage new features and functionalities for your chatbot.

TECHNOLOGY

SECTION 6
Introduction

In the rapidly evolving landscape of real estate, the path to efficient operations and optimization is *increasingly intertwined* with the adoption of advanced technology. Real estate agents and firms are discovering that leveraging technology not only streamlines processes but also enhances productivity, allowing them to scale their operations without the need for a proportional increase in staff. By integrating tools such as customer relationship management (CRM) systems, automated marketing platforms, and data analytics, agents can manage client relationships, track leads, and analyze market trends more effectively. This *technological empowerment* enables agents to focus on high-value tasks, fostering growth and innovation within their businesses.

Technology facilitates improved communication and collaboration, both internally among team members and externally with clients. Virtual tours, online listing platforms, and digital transaction management systems have transformed the way properties are marketed and sold, enabling agents to reach a broader audience with minimal effort. With the rise of artificial intelligence and machine learning, predictive analytics can provide insights into market dynamics and client preferences, allowing agents to tailor their services more precisely. This level of personalization and responsiveness is difficult to achieve with a large staff, making technology an indispensable asset for agents seeking to differentiate themselves in a competitive market.

Ultimately, *embracing technology* not only enhances operational efficiency but also positions real estate agents to respond swiftly to market changes and client needs. As the industry continues to evolve, those who harness the power of technology will find themselves at a distinct advantage, capable of growing their businesses rapidly and sustainably. By reducing reliance on an abundance of staff, agents can allocate resources more strategically, investing in technology that drives innovation and enhances the overall client experience. In this new era of real estate, the integration of technology is not just a trend, it is a foundational element for success. With these powerful tools at our disposal, the potential to build a successful and thriving business has never been greater, empowering us to innovate and scale in ways that were once unimaginable.

Technology has revolutionized the way we access and navigate information, with the creation of the *hyperlink* being a significant advancement in how we access materials. By hyperlinking items, objectives, instructions, vendors, and connections, we essentially create a web of interconnected paths that lead to various pieces of information. This interconnected web allows users to easily navigate between different sources of information, providing quick access to relevant content and resources.

Convenience: Hyperlinks allow users to access additional information or related content without leaving the current screen, saving time and effort in navigating between multiple pages or tabs.

Seamless Browsing Experience: Hyperlinks provide a seamless browsing experience by allowing users to explore relevant information within the same window, maintaining continuity in their browsing session.

Contextual Relevance: Hyperlinks enable users to access specific details or resources related to the current content they are viewing, enhancing their understanding and engagement with the topic.

Quick Access to Resources: Hyperlinks provide quick access to external sources, references, or documents without disrupting the user's flow of reading or research.

Increased Engagement: By offering clickable links within the content, users are more likely to engage with additional information, leading to a more interactive and immersive browsing experience.

Multi-Path Navigation: Hyperlinks create multiple paths for users to explore different topics, allowing them to choose their own journey through the information and discover related content easily.

Hyperlinks enhance the user experience by enabling seamless transitions between related topics, increasing efficiency in finding and accessing information. The ability to hyperlink has transformed the way we interact with digital content, making it easier to explore and discover a wealth of information and education at our fingertips.

TECHNOLOGY AND SOCIAL MEDIA

MODULE 1 | SECTION 6
Conclusion

INTEGRATE SOCIAL MEDIA AND TECHNOLOGY...

By harnessing the power of digital tools and platforms, brokers can stay ahead of the competition, adapt to changing market dynamics, and position themselves as industry leaders in delivering innovative solutions and exceptional service. The integration of technology into the real estate Industry is revolutionizing the way brokers and agents conduct business, enabling them to grow their businesses exponentially while providing top-tier service to their clients, customers, and partners. By embracing technology and leveraging its capabilities, real estate professionals can drive success, achieve operational excellence, and thrive in a competitive market landscape.

ASK YOURSELF...

- How can technology or platforms advance your marketing and branding?
- How will you use social media regularly to build, communicate, and stay engaged with your sphere?
- Who will manage your social media?
- How will you use technology, and what for in your business?
- What platforms, services, or communication can technology do more efficiently and effectively?
- How can you use technology to optimize your current business?
- How will you use AI in your business?

UNIVERSAL LAW OF RELATIVITY:

YOUR PERSPECTIVE SHAPES YOUR BUSINESS EXPERIENCES. BY VIEWING CHALLENGES AS OPPORTUNITIES FOR GROWTH, YOU CAN NAVIGATE THE REAL ESTATE MARKET WITH RESILIENCE AND ADAPTABILITY. THIS MINDSET ENABLES YOU TO TURN OBSTACLES INTO LEARNING EXPERIENCES, FOSTERING INNOVATION AND LONG-TERM SUCCESS IN YOUR ENTREPRENEURIAL JOURNEY.

BUSINESS OPERATIONS MANUAL

PARTNER POSSIBILITIES

- POSSIBLE PARTNERS INTRODUCTION
- BUSINESS LEADERSHIP POSITIONS
- POSSIBLE PARTNERS | POSITIONS
- POSSIBLE SUPPORT PARTNERSHIPS
- AGENT | OWNER | LEADER
- EXECUTIVE POSITIONS
- SUPPORT SPECIALIST ROLES

07.

MODULE 1 | SECTION 7

PARTNER POSSIBILITIES

SECTION 7
Introduction

An independent real estate agent, equipped with just one assistant, a document support person, and marketing resources, can now expand by building a team or business and scale their operations without the need to physically grow their support staff in direct proportion. Through the *utilization of technology, automation tools, and virtual assistants*, independent agents can streamline their processes, enhance efficiency, and handle a larger number of transactions effectively. By leveraging customer relationship management (CRM) systems, transaction management tools, and communication platforms, agents can manage client relationships, coordinate transactions, and collaborate with clients and team members seamlessly.

Additionally, the use of virtual assistants and *outsourcing services* allows independent agents to delegate administrative tasks, marketing activities, and other non-core functions to external professionals, freeing up their time to focus on revenue-generating activities and strategic growth initiatives. By *leveraging* virtual support, agents can access specialized expertise, scale their operations rapidly, and respond to market demands more efficiently.

This shift towards a more flexible and scalable model is making it increasingly favorable for independent agents and local teams to compete with traditional brokerage models. By harnessing the power of technology and virtual support, agents can enhance their productivity, improve client service, and expand their business without the constraints of physical office space or a large in-house team. This agile and cost-effective approach to team building is revolutionizing the real estate industry, and empowering independent agents to thrive in a competitive market, build a business, and achieve sustainable growth and success.

General Rules And Responsibilities

- General rules and responsibilities in a real estate business include maintaining ethical standards, adhering to legal regulations, providing excellent customer service, and fostering positive relationships with clients and colleagues. Clear communication, honesty, and professionalism are key aspects of these responsibilities. Keep the above in mind when choosing your support partners for your business.

Real Estate Agents

- Agents in a real estate business are responsible for representing clients in property transactions, conducting market research, negotiating deals, and staying informed about industry trends. business owners are tasked with setting strategic goals, managing finances, overseeing operations, and ensuring the overall success of the business. Leaders play a crucial role in inspiring and guiding team members, setting a positive example, and promoting a collaborative and supportive work environment. Many of the roles throughout overlap in a real estate business.

Executive Roles

- Executive Roles in a real estate business involve making high-level decisions, setting long-term objectives, developing business strategies, and overseeing the implementation of plans. Executives are responsible for driving growth, managing resources effectively, building partnerships, and ensuring the profitability and sustainability of the business.

Transaction Coordination

- Document Support Specialists in a real estate business play a vital role in organizing and maintaining important paperwork, contracts, and legal documents. They assist agents, owners, and executives in preparing and processing documentation, ensuring accuracy and compliance with regulations. Document support specialists also handle administrative tasks, manage databases, and provide essential support to streamline operations and enhance the experience.

Marketing

- Marketing support is vital in promoting properties and attracting potential buyers or renters in a competitive real estate market. Marketing professionals can help create effective campaigns, develop branding strategies, and utilize various channels to reach target audiences, ultimately driving sales and maximizing the visibility of the business.

Broker-in-Charge (BIC): Plays a crucial role in overseeing the operations, transactions, and compliance of a real estate brokerage. The BIC is responsible for ensuring that all real estate activities within the brokerage adhere to *state laws, regulations, and ethical standards*. This role may be assumed by the owner of the brokerage, a designated agent, or a specific position within the firm or company. Choosing the right Broker-in-Charge is essential for the success and reputation of the brokerage. The BIC should possess strong leadership skills, in-depth knowledge of real estate laws and practices, and a commitment to upholding ethical standards. If you do not have the expertise or experience to fulfill the role of Broker-in-Charge, it is crucial to partner with someone who possesses these qualities. Selecting a knowledgeable and trustworthy BIC can help ensure compliance, mitigate risks, and maintain the integrity of your real estate business. It is important to choose your Broker-in-Charge wisely and to establish a partnership with someone who can effectively fulfill this critical role.

Effective Operations: Plays a crucial role in ensuring *smooth and efficient business operations*. Their responsibilities encompass a wide range of tasks that are essential for the overall and success of the company. Some of the key roles and responsibilities of an operations person in a real estate company include overseeing administrative functions, managing workflow processes, coordinating communication between team members and clients, implementing and optimizing operational systems, handling logistics and project management, monitoring performance metrics, and ensuring compliance with regulations and company policies. Additionally, an operations person may be involved in strategic planning, budgeting, resource allocation, and identifying opportunities for growth and improvement. By having a highly skilled and experienced operations person in place, a real estate company can streamline its operations, enhance efficiency, and potentially replace multiple positions within the company by effectively managing various functions and responsibilities. Their ability to coordinate and optimize processes, resolve issues, and drive organizational success makes them a valuable asset in a high-functioning real estate business.

Accountant: An accountant can provide valuable insights, expertise, and support in *managing your finances effectively*. When choosing an accountant, it is important determine the level of involvement you require, whether it's basic bookkeeping, tax preparation, financial analysis, or strategic planning. By outsourcing financial tasks to a qualified accountant, you can focus on core business activities, while ensuring that your financials are accurate, organized, and compliant with regulations. Maintaining *precise financial records* not only ensures regulatory compliance but also provides a clear picture of your business's financial health and performance, enabling you to plan for growth.

In real estate, the *roles and responsibilities* of each individual agent, team or firm can vary based on their specific needs, goals, and business model. Agents may take on a variation or hybrid of tasks to fulfill their duties effectively. For example, a real estate agent may act as both a buyer's agent and a listing agent, handling transactions on both sides of the deal, as well as some or all administrative tasks. Local rules, laws, and affiliation will control much of how you are allowed to practice and represent clients in your real estate business.

Buyer's Agent: A buyer's agent represents individuals looking to purchase real estate. Tasks may include researching properties, scheduling showings, negotiating offers, and guiding clients through the buying process.

Seller's Agent: A seller's agent represents individuals looking to sell real estate. Tasks may include marketing properties, conducting open houses, negotiating offers, and assisting clients with the selling process.

Showing Assistant: A showing assistant assists real estate agents with showing properties to potential buyers. Tasks may include scheduling showings, preparing properties for viewings, and providing information to clients.

Assistant: An assistant typically provides support to a higher-level employee or team within an organization. Tasks may include scheduling appointments, organizing files, answering phone calls, and conducting research.

Front Desk: The front desk is the first point of contact for visitors or customers at a brick and mortar business or organization. Tasks may include greeting guests, answering phone calls, scheduling appointments, and providing information or assistance to visitors.

Runner: A runner typically performs various tasks such as running errands, delivering documents, and assisting with administrative duties. This role may also involve providing support to other employees within an organization.

Administration: Administration involves overseeing the day-to-day operations of a business or organization. This may include tasks such as managing office supplies, coordinating meetings, handling correspondence, and maintaining records.

Document support staff: Document support staff plays a crucial role in managing the complex process of buying or selling a property, ensuring compliance with legal requirements, and facilitating communication between all parties involved in the transaction.

Marketing: Marketing involves promoting products or services to attract customers. Tasks may include developing marketing strategies, creating advertising campaigns, conducting market research, and analyzing consumer behavior.

- **Marketing and Advertising Services:** These services help promote your listings, attract clients, and build brand awareness in the market.

- **Transaction Coordination Services or Support Staff:** Streamline the transaction process, manage paperwork, and ensure smooth transactions for clients.

- **Technology Providers**: Tech partners offer tools for virtual tours, digital marketing, data analytics, and process automation.

- **Networking and Industry Connections:** Building relationships with other real estate professionals, industry experts, and local businesses can lead to referrals and collaborations.

- **Printing and Shipping:** Partnering with a local company for printing and shipping can be beneficial to agents, partners, and sellers.

- **CRM:** Customer Relationship Management software helps manage client relationships, track leads, and streamline communication.

- **Financial Services:** Accountants, financial advisors, and lenders help with financial planning, budgeting, and mortgage services.

- **Legal Services:** Legal partners and vendors provide guidance on real estate laws, contracts, and compliance issues.

- **Title and Escrow Companies:** Partners in title and escrow services facilitate the closing process and ensure a smooth transfer of ownership.

- **Home Inspection Services:** Inspection vendors ensure properties meet safety and quality standards, providing peace of mind to clients.

- **Photography and Videography Services:** Visual content creators help showcase properties through high-quality images and videos.

- **Branded Office and Apparel Supply Services and Vendors:** Connecting with a partnered vendor for branded appreciation gifts can help streamline individual, and business operations while adding an extra level of service.

- **Signature Platform | Company Information | Documents:** Signature platforms help simplify the process and time needed to prepare and sign documents.

- **Agent Onboarding:** Partnered onboarding services can help support and simplify the onboarding process for new agents and the business, team or firm.

Team Leader:

A team leader in a real estate team is responsible for *overseeing and managing* a group of agents or team members. Their role involves providing guidance, support, and direction to team members to help them achieve their individual and collective goals. Responsibilities may include setting team objectives, developing strategies to meet sales targets, monitoring team performance, providing training and coaching, and fostering a positive and collaborative team culture. The team leader plays a crucial role in ensuring the success and productivity of the team.

Owner of a Real Estate Team:

The owner of a real estate team is responsible for the *overall management and success* of the team. Their role involves setting the vision and direction for the team, making strategic decisions to grow the business, and ensuring that the team operates efficiently and profitably. Responsibilities may include setting business goals and objectives, developing business plans and budgets, overseeing team operations, hiring and managing team members, and building relationships with clients and industry partners. The owner plays a key role in driving the long-term success and sustainability of the real estate team.

Top Producer:

In the context of a real estate team, this position is a *top-producing agent or team member* who consistently generates a significant amount of business and revenue for the team. A top producer is often responsible for bringing in new clients, securing listings, and closing deals at a high volume. Their role is crucial in driving the financial success and growth of the team. Responsibilities may include prospecting for new business, building and maintaining client relationships, negotiating contracts, and staying updated on market trends and opportunities.

Independent Agent / Broker :

An independent agent / broker with *no employees or affiliation* is responsible for managing all aspects of their real estate business independently. This includes acquiring clients, negotiating contracts, marketing properties, handling administrative tasks, and ensuring compliance with legal and ethical standards. The agent broker must also maintain relationships with clients and industry contacts, stay updated on market trends and regulations, and continuously seek opportunities to grow their business. Additionally, they are accountable for financial management, budgeting, and decision-making to sustain and expand their real estate operations successfully.

CEO (Chief Executive Officer): The CEO is the highest-ranking executive in a real estate company and is responsible for making *major* corporate decisions, managing overall operations, and implementing strategies to achieve the company's goals. Tasks may include setting company objectives, leading the executive team, representing the company to stakeholders, and overseeing the company's financial performance.

Executive Assistant: An executive assistant provides *administrative support* to top executives in a real estate company, such as the CEO, CFO, or COO. Tasks may include managing schedules, coordinating meetings, handling correspondence, preparing reports, and assisting with special projects. Executive assistants play a crucial role in ensuring the smooth operation of the executive's office and supporting their daily activities.

COO (Chief Operating Officer): The COO is responsible for *overseeing the day-to-day operations* of a real estate company and ensuring that business operations are running efficiently. Tasks may include developing operational strategies, managing operational processes, optimizing business performance, and *implementing* policies and procedures to improve productivity.

CFO (Chief Financial Officer): The CFO is responsible for managing the *financial aspects* of a real estate company, including financial planning, budgeting, and financial reporting. Tasks may include analyzing financial data, developing financial strategies, managing investments, overseeing financial controls, and ensuring compliance with financial regulations.

As a real estate business owner, team owner, franchise operator, or large firm operator, there are numerous *moving pieces and parts* that require careful management and coordination to ensure smooth operations and success. These moving components may include multiple agents and brokers, various properties and listings, client relationships, marketing and advertising strategies, financial transactions, legal compliance, technology systems, administrative tasks, and more. Each of these elements plays a crucial role in the overall functioning of the business, and it is essential for the owner to oversee and optimize these moving parts effectively. By implementing efficient processes, clear communication channels, robust systems, and strategic planning, a real estate business owner can streamline operations, enhance productivity, and drive growth and profitability within their organization.

Transaction Coordinator: A transaction coordinator is responsible for managing the *administrative aspects* of a real estate transaction from contract to close. Tasks may include coordinating communication between buyers, sellers, agents, and other parties involved in the transaction, ensuring all necessary documents are completed and signed, scheduling inspections and appraisals, and ensuring that all deadlines are met. The transaction coordinator helps to ensure a smooth and timely closing process.

Buyers Support Specialist: A buyers support specialist provides *administrative support* to real estate agents who are working *with buyers* to find and purchase properties. Tasks may include conducting property searches, scheduling showings, preparing purchase agreements, coordinating inspections and appraisals, and assisting with the closing process. The buyers support specialist helps to ensure that the buyer's needs are met and that the transaction progresses smoothly.

Listing Support Specialist: A listing support specialist provides *administrative support* to real estate agents who are *listing properties* for sale. Tasks may include preparing listing agreements, creating marketing materials, coordinating photography and virtual tours, inputting listings into the MLS (Multiple Listing Service), scheduling showings, and assisting with open houses. The listing support specialist helps to ensure that the property is effectively marketed to potential buyers.

When roles and responsibilities are clearly documented and structured within any real estate business, it can create a *highly efficient operational system*. This documentation helps to outline the connection points and workflow between tasks, ensuring that each team member understands their responsibilities and how they fit into the larger picture of the agency's operations. For Example: A marketing team may be responsible for creating advertising campaigns and promoting properties, while the administration team handles scheduling appointments and maintaining records. The buyer's agent and seller's agent work together to guide clients through the buying and selling process, with support from showing assistants and runners who assist with property showings and administrative tasks. With the use of technology, many professionals are now taking on the roles of multiple positions, reducing the number of positions needed to efficiently and effectively grow your business.

PARTNER POSSIBILITIES

MODULE 1 | SECTION 7
Conclusion

ROLES | RESPONSIBILITIES...

Assistants, partners, and virtual staff plays a crucial role in managing the complex process of buying or selling a property, ensuring compliance with legal requirements, facilitating communication between all parties involved in the transaction, creating content, marketing efforts, and managing customer relations. Work through the list of support services that you may need or want to add, and add additional support options that may fit your model. Once you have chosen the pieces and parts you will use for support, you will need to clarify how each service or provider may connect or interact.

ASK YOURSELF...

- What partners or staff do you use to power your business?

- What partners or staff could benefit you as you grow and expand?

- How will you document your partner or staff roles, responsibilities, or expectations?

- What positions or partners can use technology to optimize your process?

BUSINESS OPERATIONS MANUAL

EXEMPLARY SERVICE

- EXEMPLARY SERVICE INTRODUCTION
- THE EXTRAS | CLIENT TEMPLATES
- KEY COMMUNICATION OPPORTUNITIES
- SELLER / BUYER | COMMUNICATION OPPORTUNITIES
- OPEN HOUSE ITEMS YOU MAY NEED
- HOST A CREATIVE OPEN HOUSE
- CLIENT GRATITUDE AND APPRECIATION
- NEWSLETTERS | IDEAS TO CONNECT
- MAIL YOUR BRANDED MATERIALS
- MONTHLY TARGET MARKETING
- POTENTIAL SELLER PARTNERSHIP
- AGENT CELEBRATION OPPORTUNITIES
- THOUGHTFUL GESTURES
- LOCAL EXPERIENCES
- PROPERTY TRANSFER INFORMATION
- UTILITY TRANSFER INFORMATION
- MOVING CHECKLIST

08.

MODULE 1 | SECTION 8

EXEMPLARY SERVICE

SECTION 8
Introduction

In the real estate industry, providing exceptional service is key to building strong relationships with clients and partners, while also growing your business. There are numerous ways to go above and beyond in servicing your clients and partners. Branded marketing companies, virtual connection platforms, and creative strategies can help you stand out in a competitive market. By offering *unique and personalized experiences*, you can create a lasting impression and foster loyalty among your clients and partners. By focusing on providing exceptional service, leveraging creative strategies, and nurturing authentic relationships, you can differentiate yourself in the real estate market, build a strong reputation, and ultimately grow your business through satisfied clients and loyal partners.

In today's rapidly evolving marketplace, real estate agents and business owners must embrace *creativity and innovation* to differentiate themselves and thrive. By exploring unconventional service solutions, such as leveraging technology for enhanced customer experiences, personalizing client interactions, and developing unique marketing strategies, professionals can unlock new opportunities for growth and engagement. Encouraging a culture of *experimentation and open-mindedness* allows teams to think outside the box, adapt to changing market demands, and anticipate client needs before they arise. Ultimately, those who are willing to push the boundaries of traditional practices will not only build stronger relationships with their clients but also position themselves as leaders in their industry, paving the way for sustained success and a competitive edge.

When clients feel valued and supported at every touchpoint, they are more likely to become repeat customers, advocating for your brand. By shifting the focus from relentless pursuit to nurturing and enhancing current relationships, agents can build a loyal client base that not only sustains their business but also drives organic growth through positive word-of-mouth.

PROVIDING EXEMPLARY SERVICE

Creating and *documenting* your company and client services and standards is a crucial and rewarding aspect of building a real estate business, as it establishes consistency, enhances professionalism, and fosters trust with clients.

Branded Marketing Companies:

Partnering with branded marketing companies to provide thoughtful and personalized gifts for your clients and partners can show appreciation and gratitude in a meaningful way. Whether it's a closing gift, a holiday present, or a token of gratitude, thoughtful gifts can leave a lasting impression and strengthen your relationships.

Virtual Connection Companies:

Utilizing virtual connection platforms can help you stay connected with clients and partners, especially in today's digital age where virtual communication is increasingly important. Virtual meetings, webinars, and online events can provide a convenient and efficient way to engage with clients and partners, regardless of location.

Creative Service Strategies:

Implementing creative service strategies, such as hosting client appreciation events, organizing educational workshops, or offering exclusive perks and benefits, can help differentiate your business and create a unique customer experience. By thinking outside the box and providing value-added services, you can build trust, loyalty, and long-term relationships with your clients and partners.

Build Authentic Relationships:

Building authentic relationships through maintaining high-level and consistent service standards is essential for success in the real estate industry. By prioritizing exceptional service and consistently exceeding expectations, you can establish yourself as a trusted and reliable partner in the eyes of your clients and partners. Authentic relationships built on trust, communication, and mutual respect are more likely to lead to repeat business, referrals, and long-term success in the industry.

In the real estate industry, providing exceptional service can set you apart from the competition and leave a lasting impression on your clients. By incorporating simple acts of service and thoughtful touches throughout the transaction process, you can enhance the overall experience for your customers and build stronger relationships. Here are some items that you can add to create exceptional service:

Local Service Providers Sheet:
Providing clients with a list of recommended local service providers, such as contractors, inspectors, movers, and landscapers, can be incredibly helpful. This sheet can serve as a valuable resource for clients who may need assistance with home maintenance, repairs, or renovations after purchasing a property.

Seller Property Information Sheet:
Creating a detailed property information sheet for sellers can help them showcase their home's features and amenities effectively. This sheet can include key details about the property, such as square footage, upgrades, recent renovations, a floor plan, and neighborhood highlights, to attract potential buyers and generate interest in the listing.

Offer Cover Sheet For Submitting An Offer:
Including an offer cover sheet when submitting an offer on a property can add a personal touch and make your offer stand out. This sheet can summarize the offer terms, buyer's qualifications, and any additional information that may strengthen the offer and demonstrate the buyer's commitment to the transaction.

Offer Instructions Sheet For Submitting An Offer:
Providing clear instructions for agents and clients on the requirements and steps involved in submitting an offer can streamline the process and alleviate any confusion or uncertainty. This sheet can outline the necessary documents, deadlines, and procedures for submitting an offer, ensuring that agents and clients are well-prepared and informed throughout the transaction.

By incorporating these items into your real estate transactions, you can demonstrate your commitment to exceptional service, enhance the overall experience for your clients, and build trust and loyalty in your relationships. These simple acts of service can go a long way in creating a positive and memorable experience for your clients, setting you apart as a trusted and reliable real estate professional in your local market.

As a real estate agent, it's essential to create unique touch points or *specific opportunities* for communication in your clients' journey in order to build strong connections and leave a lasting impression. These touch points can enhance the client experience, strengthen relationships, and differentiate your brand in a competitive market. Here are some key communication opportunities and ways to celebrate them:

Key Communication Opportunity 1 : Clients First Connection

Client's First Connection: Make a memorable first impression by sending a personalized welcome message, handwritten note, or small gift to new clients. This gesture shows your appreciation for their trust in choosing you as their agent and sets a positive tone for the relationship.

Key Communication Opportunity 2 : Property Just Listed

Property Just Listed: When a new property is listed, showcase it in a creative and engaging way through social media posts, virtual tours, or personalized property brochures. Keep clients informed and excited about the listing, demonstrating your proactive approach to marketing their property.

Key Communication Opportunity 3 : Property Under Contract

Offer Accepted: Celebrate the moment when an offer is accepted by sending a congratulatory message, arranging a virtual toast, or organizing a small gift delivery to mark this significant milestone in the transaction process. This shows your clients that you are invested in their success and share in their joy.

Key Communication Opportunity 4 : Property Closed

Property Closed: After the successful closing of a property, express your gratitude and appreciation to clients with a thoughtful closing gift, a handwritten thank-you note, or a personalized closing ceremony. This final touchpoint reinforces your commitment to providing exceptional service and fosters long-term relationships with clients.

As a team owner, firm operator, or business owner, it is equally important to create unique and identifiable communication opportunities and moments to celebrate your partners. Recognizing their achievements, milestones, and contributions through personalized gestures, team events, or incentives can boost morale, motivation, and loyalty within your team. By acknowledging their support, trust, and collaboration through personalized connections and meaningful gestures, you build strong relationships, foster loyalty, and establish your reputation as a trusted and valued partner in the real estate industry. These unique moments of celebration and appreciation not only enhance the client and agent experience but also contribute to the long-term success and sustainability of your business.

Key Communication Opportunity 1:
Listing Agreement Signed: Celebrate when the home seller signs the listing agreement, marking the official start of the selling process and demonstrating their trust in your services.

Key Communication Opportunity 2:
Professional Photography Session: Celebrate when professional photography is done to showcase the property in its best light, enhancing its appeal and attracting potential buyers.

Key Communication Opportunity 3:
Listing Goes Live: Celebrate when the listing goes live on the market, reaching a wider audience and generating interest from potential buyers.

Key Communication Opportunity 4:
Open House: Celebrate hosting a successful open house, providing a chance for interested buyers to view the property and potentially make an offer.

Key Communication Opportunity 5:
Offer Received: Celebrate when the seller receives an offer on their property, indicating interest from a potential buyer and moving closer to a successful sale.

Key Communication Opportunity 6:
Offer Accepted: Celebrate when the seller accepts an offer, solidifying the deal and moving towards the closing process.

Key Communication Opportunity 7:
Home Inspection: Celebrate when the home inspection is completed, ensuring that the property meets the necessary requirements and addressing any issues that may arise.

Key Communication Opportunity 8:
Closing Day: Celebrate when the sale is finalized, and the property is officially transferred to the new owner, marking the successful completion.

Key Communication Opportunity 1:
Initial Consultation: Celebrate the initial consultation with the home buyer, where you discuss their needs, preferences, and goals for buying a home, marking the beginning of the home buying process and establishing a strong client-agent relationship.

Key Communication Opportunity 2:
Pre-Approval: Celebrate when the home buyer obtains pre-approval for a mortgage, demonstrating their financial readiness to purchase a home and narrowing down their search criteria.

Key Communication Opportunity 3:
Offer Accepted: Celebrate when the home buyer's offer on a property is accepted by the seller signaling a significant milestone in the home buying process and moving closer to closing the deal.

Key Communication Opportunity 4:
Home Inspection: Celebrate when the home inspection is completed, ensuring that the property meets the necessary standards and addressing any issues that may arise, providing peace of mind to the home buyer.

Key Communication Opportunity 5:
Appraisal: Celebrate when the property appraisal is conducted, determining the fair market value of the home and confirming that the purchase price aligns with the property's worth.

Key Communication Opportunity 6:
Loan Approval: Celebrate when the home buyer's mortgage loan is approved by the lender, securing the necessary financing to purchase the home and moving towards the closing phase.

Key Communication Opportunity 7:
Final Walkthrough: Celebrate when the home buyer conducts a final walkthrough of the property before closing, ensuring that everything is in order and meeting their expectations before taking ownership.

Key Communication Opportunity 8:
Closing Day: Celebrate when the home buyer completes the closing process, signs the necessary paperwork, and officially takes possession of the property, marking the successful completion of the home buying journey.

ITEMS :

Open House Event

1. Signage and Directional Signs
2. Property Information Sheets and Brochures
3. Business Cards and Contact Information
4. Guest Book or Sign-In Sheet
5. Refreshments and Snacks
6. Cleaning Supplies and Trash Bins
7. Music or Background Ambiance
8. Comfortable Seating Areas
9. Property Features Checklist
10. Virtual Tour Equipment (if applicable)
11. Hand Sanitizer
12. Gift Bags or Giveaways
13. Open House Feedback Forms
14. Outdoor Decorations or Landscaping
15. Marketing Materials and Signage
16. MLS Sheets or Any Specific Documents
17. Property Marketing Book | Details
18. Branded Giveaways
19. CMA Sheets for Potential Sellers
20. Interactive Tools | I Pad | Sound Machine

INVENTORY:

Open House | Office

- Plates
- Cups
- Bowls
- Silverware
- Napkins
- Skewers
- Serving Platters
- Serving Bowls
- Cutting Boards
- Champagne Glasses
- Wine Glasses
- Wine Bottle Opener

ATTACH:
Information and Details

Ordering Links
[Office Inventory]

Company Storage Links|
Sign in sheets or materials
[Location Link]

Company Process|
Open House Policies
[Attached]

Standard Communication|
Template for follow up
[Attached]

As you plan your open house or event do not forget to attach a *staple list of things* that will or could be needed. Attach links for any template access, passwords, or contact person for ordering while building your operations. Keeping these essentials in an organized manner keeps things effective and efficient for both the agent and the team or firm.

By hosting a *creative and engaging* open house, you can create a positive and memorable experience for attendees, build relationships with potential clients, and differentiate yourself from competitors in the market. Additionally, a successful open house can help you generate leads, gather valuable feedback, and establish yourself as a trusted and knowledgeable real estate Professional.

- **Virtual Open House:** Host a virtual tour of the property using live video streaming or virtual reality technology to reach a wider audience and engage potential buyers who may not be able to attend in person.

- **Themed Open House:** Decorate the property based on a specific theme such as a seasonal holiday, a popular movie or TV show, or a local event to create a memorable experience for visitors.

- **Interactive Activities:** Incorporate interactive elements such as games, contests, or raffles to keep attendees engaged and encourage participation.

- **Food and Beverage Stations:** Offer refreshments, snacks, or a coffee bar to create a welcoming and hospitable atmosphere for visitors.

- **Local Vendor Showcase:** Partner with local businesses or vendors to showcase their products or services at the open house, creating a sense of community and supporting local businesses.

- **DIY Home Improvement Workshops:** Host DIY workshops or demonstrations on home improvement projects, staging tips, or interior design ideas to educate and inspire attendees.

- **Outdoor Entertainment:** Set up outdoor seating areas, lawn games, or a barbecue station to create a relaxed and inviting outdoor space for visitors to enjoy.

- **Personalized Property Brochures:** Create custom property brochures with high-quality photos, detailed descriptions, and floor plans to provide attendees with comprehensive information about the Property.

- **Virtual Reality Tours:** Offer virtual reality tours of the property using VR headsets to provide an immersive and interactive experience for visitors.

- **Gift Bags | Giveaways:** Provide attendees with branded gift bags, promotional items, or personalized giveaways as a token of appreciation for visiting the open house.

By hosting client appreciation events, real estate agents can build stronger relationships, create a positive experience for clients, and differentiate themselves in a competitive market. These events not only show gratitude to clients but also help agents stay connected, generate referrals, and grow their network.

Housewarming Party: Throw a housewarming party for clients who have recently purchased a home. This can be a fun way to celebrate their new home and create a sense of community.

Homebuyer Seminar: Host a seminar or workshop for homebuyers to provide valuable information on the home buying process, market trends, financing options, and tips for a successful purchase.

Wine Tasting Event: Organize a wine tasting event at a local winery or wine bar for clients to enjoy an evening of wine tasting, networking, and socializing.

BBQ or Picnic: Host a BBQ or picnic in a park or outdoor venue for clients to enjoy good food, games, and a relaxed atmosphere.

Client Appreciation Dinner: Treat your clients to a special dinner at a local restaurant or event venue to show your appreciation for their business.

Movie Night: Organize a movie night at a local theater or outdoor screening with popcorn, snacks, and a movie selection that appeals to your clients.

Networking Mixer: Host a networking mixer or happy hour event for clients to connect with other professionals in the community and expand their network.

Educational Workshop: Offer an educational workshop on topics such as home maintenance, interior design, or real estate investing to provide value to your clients.

Charity Event: Partner with a local charity or non-profit organization to host a charity event or fundraiser that allows clients to give back to the community.

Seasonal Celebration: Host a seasonal celebration such as a holiday party, summer BBQ, or fall festival to bring clients together and celebrate the season.

Choose from the list above, or come up with your own *creative and unique* appreciation events! Be sure to document the details of each event, process, materials, and vendors. This will allow you to assess and adjust for future events.

Sending out a monthly newsletter to your sphere of influence can be a valuable tool for maintaining relationships and staying connected with your contacts. By consistently providing something of value in your newsletter, whether it's market updates, real estate tips, community news, or personal anecdotes, you can keep your audience engaged and interested in what you have to say.

- **Client Success Stories:** Highlight successful transactions or testimonials from satisfied clients.
- **Local Market Updates:** Provide insights and trends in the local real estate market.
- **Home Improvement Tips:** Share DIY projects, renovation ideas, or home staging tips.
- **Neighborhood Spotlights:** Showcase different neighborhoods, highlighting amenities, events, and attractions.
- **Real Estate News:** Share industry news, market trends, and updates.
- **Seasonal Home Maintenance Checklist:** Provide a checklist of tasks to maintain a home throughout the year.
- **Featured Listings:** Showcase current listings with high-quality photos and descriptions.
- **Real Estate Investing Tips:** Share tips and strategies for real estate investors.
- **Community Events:** Highlight upcoming events, festivals, or activities in the area.
- **Mortgage Tips:** Provide information on mortgage rates, loan options, and financing tips.
- **Home Buyer/Seller Tips:** Offer advice for buyers and sellers on navigating the real estate process.
- **Interior Design Inspiration:** Share interior design trends, decorating tips, and inspiration.
- **Virtual Tours:** Create virtual tours of properties to showcase to clients.

- **Home Safety Tips:** Offer tips on home security, fire safety, and emergency preparedness.
- **Local Business Features:** Spotlight local businesses, restaurants, or service providers.
- **Real Estate Glossary:** Define common real estate terms and jargon for clients.
- **Client Appreciation Events:** Invite clients to special events or webinars to show appreciation.
- **Real estate market Predictions:** Share insights and predictions for the future of the real estate market.
- **Home Buying/Selling Process:** Break down the steps involved in buying or selling a home.
- **Energy Efficiency Tips:** Provide tips on saving energy, reducing utility bills, and eco-friendly living.
- **Home Organization Ideas:** Share tips for decluttering, organizing, and maximizing space in a home.
- **Industry Expert Interviews:** Interview industry experts, real estate agents, or home professionals for insights.
- **Real Estate Trivia:** Create a fun trivia section related to real estate facts and history.
- **Client Connection Program:** Promote a connection program for clients to earn an invitation to a monthly or quarterly networking event for referring new business.

This regular communication helps to nurture relationships, build trust, and position yourself as a knowledgeable and reliable resource in the real estate Industry. By consistently providing valuable content and staying connected through regular communication, you can strengthen your relationships, foster loyalty, and ultimately grow your business through repeat and referral business from your sphere of influence. Above is a list of topics to help get you started with your monthly connections!

WINTER:

Customized knit beanies: Branded beanies with your company logo are practical and stylish winter accessories that can be worn by clients or employees.

Personalized hot chocolate kits: Create custom hot chocolate kits with branded mugs, hot chocolate mix, and marshmallows for a cozy winter treat.

Branded fleece blankets: Customized fleece blankets with your logo are warm and comforting gifts that can be used during the colder months.

SPRING:

Customized reusable tote bags: Branded tote bags with spring-themed designs can be practical and eco-friendly giveaways for clients or employees.

Personalized seed packets: Create custom seed packets with your company branding for clients to plant and grow their own flowers or herbs in the spring.

Branded sunglasses: Custom sunglasses with your logo are stylish and practical items that can be worn during the sunny spring days.

SUMMER:

Customized beach towels: Branded beach towels with your company logo are practical items for clients to use at the beach or pool during the summer.

Personalized insulated water bottles: Create custom insulated water bottles with your branding for clients to stay hydrated during the hot summer months.

Branded sunscreen: Custom sunscreen bottles with your logo are practical and thoughtful giveaways for clients to protect their skin during the summer.

FALL:

Customized cozy socks: Branded cozy socks with fall-themed designs are warm and comfortable gifts for clients or employees to wear during the autumn season.

Personalized pumpkin spice candles: Create custom pumpkin spice candles with your company branding for a festive and seasonal gift.

Branded travel mugs: Custom travel mugs with your logo are practical items for clients to enjoy their favorite hot beverages on-the-go.

Personalizing your branded marketing materials for your clients and partners can make a significant impact on their engagement and receptiveness to your message. By tailoring your materials to reflect the *individual preferences, interests, or needs* of your target audience, you can create a more meaningful and memorable experience for them. This personal touch shows that you have taken time and effort to understand their unique preferences and cater to their specific needs, making them feel valued and appreciated.

BRANDED ITEMS EASILY PERSONALIZED:

Branded Apparel: Clothing items such as t-shirts, hats, or jackets with your company logo can serve as walking advertisements for your brand when worn by employees or given as promotional items.

Customized Drink-Ware: Branded mugs, water bottles, or tumblers are practical items that can be used daily, providing continuous exposure for your business.

Promotional Bags: Tote bags, backpacks, and laptop bags with your company logo are useful and versatile marketing items that can be used for shopping, travel, or everyday activities, showcasing your brand wherever they go.

Branded Tech Accessories: Items such as phone cases, laptop sleeves, or power banks with your logo are practical and popular items that can be used by customers on a daily basis, increasing brand visibility.

Customized Stationery: Notebooks, pens, or sticky notes with your business name and logo are practical and cost-effective marketing items that can be used in various settings.

MAKE IT PERSONAL:

Color: Choosing a gift in the recipient's favorite color adds a personal touch and shows that you have considered their preferences.

Smell: Selecting a scented gift such as candles, perfumes, or bath products in a scent that the recipient enjoys can evoke positive emotions and memories.

Taste: Giving a gift of gourmet food or beverages that align with the recipient's taste preferences can be a delightful and indulgent treat.

Personalization: Adding a monogram, name, or special message to a gift through engraving, embroidery, or custom printing makes it unique and meaningful.

Hobby or Interest: Selecting a gift related to the recipient's hobbies, interests, or passions shows that you have taken the time to consider their individual preferences, making it personal.

BUILDING YOUR BRAND:

Create a list of branded materials you will use for your business | Include small items that can be easily mailed:

- **Customized Pens:** Pens with your business name and logo are practical and cost-effective marketing items that can be used in various settings, providing continuous brand exposure.
- **Branded Notebooks:** Notebooks with your company logo are useful and portable marketing tools that can be given to clients, employees, or at events to promote your brand.
- **Customized Keychains:** Keychains with your business name or logo are inexpensive promotional items that can be distributed at trade shows, events, or as part of a customer campaign.
- **Logo Stickers:** Stickers with your company logo can be affixed to laptops, notebooks, water bottles, or other items, increasing brand visibility and awareness.
- **Branded Tote Bags:** Tote bags with your business logo are practical and eco-friendly marketing items that can be used for shopping, travel, or everyday activities, showcasing your brand wherever they go.
- **Customized Magnets:** Magnets with your company logo can be placed on refrigerators or other metal surfaces, serving as a constant reminder of your brand to customers.
- **Personalized USB Drives:** USB drives with your business name and logo are useful and memorable marketing items that can be pre-loaded with promotional materials or information about your business or services.
- **Personalized Postcards:** Postcards with your company branding and a personalized message can be sent to clients or prospects, adding a personal touch to your marketing efforts.
- **Customized Bookmarks:** Bookmarks with your logo can be mailed to customers or included as a promotional item with purchases, keeping your brand in the mind of the client during reading sessions.
- **Flat Beverage Opener:** A flat bottle or beverage opener can be mailed easily, and stored in a wallet or purse, turning your brand into a useful tool.

With the use of technology, real estate professionals can schedule posts, emails, and various connection points ahead of time, allowing for efficient and timely communication with clients and prospects. By *leveraging scheduling tools and automation features*, agents can plan and schedule their outreach efforts in advance, ensuring consistent and strategic engagement with their sphere of influence. Taking the time to populate holiday posts and other relevant content ahead of time has revolutionized how real estate professionals connect with their sphere. This proactive approach not only saves time and effort but also ensures that agents maintain a consistent presence and stay top of mind with their audience.

CREATE A SYSTEM FOR YOUR MONTHLY MARKETING:

Use the following system and list of dates, or create your own system to connect regularly with your monthly target marketing plan. Be creative!

MONTHLY		
1st Day	1. New Year's Day	1. January 1st
	2. Valentine's Day	2. February 14th
	3. St. Patrick's Day	3. March 17th
15th Day	4. Easter Sunday	4. First Sunday in April (Varies)
	5. Mother's Day	5. Second Sunday in May
	6. Memorial Day	6. Last Monday in May
Last Day	7. Father's Day	7. Third Sunday in June
	8. Independence Day	8. July 4th
Holidays	9. Labor Day	9. First Monday in September
	10. Halloween	10. October 31st
	11. Thanksgiving Day	11. Fourth Thursday in November
	12. Christmas Day	12. December 25th

Client appreciation events around holidays provide a great *opportunity to get creative* and connect with clients on a personal level. By incorporating holiday themes and activities into your events, you can create memorable experiences that show your clients how much you *value* their business and relationship. For example, you can host a pie giveaway for Thanksgiving, where clients can pick up a delicious pie to enjoy with their loved ones. For Halloween, consider organizing a trunk- or-treat event for kids in the community, providing a safe and fun environment for families to celebrate the holiday. Another idea is to offer photos during the holiday season, giving families the chance to capture special memories and create a festive atmosphere. Some seasonal branded gift ideas to consider are listed below:

1.Customized Holiday Ornaments:
Personalized ornaments with your company logo can be a festive and memorable seasonal gift for clients or employees.

2.Seasonal Candles:
Branded candles in seasonal scents can create a cozy and welcoming atmosphere, making them a thoughtful gift for recipients.

3.Winter Accessories:
Branded scarves, gloves, or hats are practical items that can be customized with your logo and sent out as seasonal gifts.

4.Seasonal Treats:
Customized cookies, chocolates, or other seasonal treats can be a sweet and delicious way to spread holiday cheer and promote your brand.

5.Seasonal Stationary:
Personalized holiday cards, calendars, or notepads with your company branding can be useful items that recipients can enjoy throughout the year.

When working with a *potential seller*, it is crucial to provide value and demonstrate expertise to build trust and confidence in your services. By laying out a clear plan and explaining the value you bring to the table, you can help potential seller clients understand the *benefits* of partnering with you as their real estate agent. This may include providing a comparative market analysis, staging advice, professional photography, marketing and advertising strategies, negotiation expertise, and guidance throughout the selling process. Below is a list of services that may help you partner with a potential seller.

1. Offer a Free Home Valuation: Provide a complimentary home valuation to potential seller clients to demonstrate your expertise and market knowledge.

2. Share Market Insights: Provide potential seller clients with market trends, statistics, and insights to help them make informed decisions.

3. Offer Marketing Tips: Share tips and strategies for effectively marketing their property, such as staging, photography, and online listings.

4. Provide Resources: Offer resources such as professional photographers, home stagers, or contractors to assist potential seller clients in preparing their property for sale.

5. Host a Virtual Open House: Organize a virtual open house for potential seller clients to showcase their property to a wider audience and attract potential buyers.

6. Create a Custom Marketing Plan: Develop a personalized marketing plan outlining strategies to promote the potential sellers property and reach potential buyers.

7. Offer Negotiation Support: Provide the value of a listing agent when negotiating offers and closing the deal with potential buyers.

8. Share Testimonials: Share success stories and testimonials from previous clients to build credibility and trust with potential seller clients.

9. Provide Market Updates: Keep potential seller clients informed about changes in the real estate market and how it may impact their selling process.

10. Offer a Partnership: Propose a partnership where you work together with the potential partner client to market and sell their property, leveraging your expertise and resources with a formalized agreement.

By clearly communicating your plan and services, you can demonstrate your commitment to providing *exceptional value and support* to potential clients. This transparency and professionalism can help build rapport, establish trust, and ultimately lead to a successful partnership in selling their property.

PERSONAL MILESTONES | AGENT PARTNER KEY COMMUNICATION OPPORTUNITIES
[Agent Birthday]   [Top Producer | Goal Reached]   [Work Anniversary | Year 1 / 5 / 10]

Key Communication Opportunity 1| First Sale:
Celebrate your first successful sale as a real estate agent, as it marks the beginning of your career and the start of a successful business.

Key Communication Opportunity 2| Closing a High-Value Deal:
Celebrate closing a high-value deal, whether it's a luxury property, commercial real estate transaction, or a significant investment opportunity.

Key Communication Opportunity 3| Reaching a Sales Goal:
Celebrate reaching a specific sales goal, such as closing a certain number of transactions in a month, quarter, or year.

Key Communication Opportunity 4| Winning an Award:
Celebrate receiving recognition or an award for your performance, such as being a top producer in your brokerage or earning a prestigious industry award.

Key Communication Opportunity 5| Closing a Difficult Deal:
Celebrate successfully closing a challenging deal that required extra effort, negotiation skills, and perseverance.

Key Communication Opportunity 6| Growing Your Client Base: Celebrate expanding your client base and attracting new leads and referrals through your marketing efforts and networking activities.

Key Communication Opportunity 7| Achieving a Certification or Designation:
Celebrate earning a professional certification or designation, such as becoming a Certified Residential Specialist (CRS) or Accredited Buyer's Representative (ABR).

Key Communication Opportunity 8| Achieving a Social Media Milestone:
Celebrate reaching a milestone on social media, such as gaining a certain number of followers, engagement on posts, or positive reviews from clients.

Key Communication Opportunity 9| Hosting a Successful Client Appreciation Event:
Celebrate hosting a successful client appreciation event that strengthens relationships with clients, generates referrals, and showcases your expertise and professionalism.

Key Communication Opportunity 10| Personal Growth Milestones:
Celebrate personal growth milestones, such as improving your negotiation skills, mastering a new technology or marketing strategy, or overcoming a fear or challenge in your business.

Creating a personalized agent retention program for your business, employees, or team can be a valuable way to show appreciation and enhance employee satisfaction. By recognizing and celebrating key moments such as birthdays, work anniversaries, special achievements, or personal milestones, you demonstrate that you *value your agents* as individuals and acknowledge their contributions to the team. Personalized gestures such as handwritten notes, small gifts, or thoughtful gestures can make employees feel valued and appreciated, boosting morale and fostering a positive work environment. This personalized approach helps to build loyalty and strengthen relationships within the team, leading to higher retention rates and a more engaged and motivated workforce. By investing in your agents and showing that you care about their well- being, you can create a supportive and inclusive workplace culture that benefits both employees and the overall success of the business.

1. Succulent plants in decorative pots

2. Customized keychains with the agent's initials or home address

3. Gourmet cookies or baked goods from a local bakery

4. Personalized notepads or stationery sets

5. A small bottle of wine or champagne with a branded wine stopper

6. A set of scented candles in seasonal fragrances

7. Local artisanal honey or jam with a custom label

8. Mini herb garden kits for agents with a green thumb

9. Cozy throw blankets or decorative pillows for the home

10. A selection of gourmet coffee or tea packaged in a gift basket

Creating a list of your local favorites can be a *valuable resource* for setting your clients up for success, especially if they are visiting from out of town. By curating a list of recommended restaurants, attractions, activities, and services in your area, you can help your clients make the most of their visit and ensure a positive experience during their stay. Providing insider tips and personalized recommendations can enhance their overall impression of the area and leave a lasting impression.

In today's digital age, sharing your list of local favorites is easier than ever. You can create a digital document, a dedicated webpage, or even a social media post with your recommendations to encourage client engagement. By providing this personalized touch, you demonstrate your local expertise, thoughtfulness, and commitment to ensuring your clients have a positive experience. Ultimately, by sharing your local favorites, you can add value to your client relationships, showcase your knowledge of the area, and help your clients make the most of their visit.

- Local Restaurants and Dinning
- Local Coffee Shops / Tea Shops
- Local Sweet Treats
- Local Hotels and Lodging
- Local / Historic Attractions
- Local Outdoor / Adventures
- Local Malls
- Local Shopping
- Local Art
- Local and Unique Furniture Shopping
- Local Romantic Attractions
- Event Centers / Venues
- Rental Company Connections | Home / Cars

SELLERS TRANSFER INFORMATION

Entrance
Gate Code
Entrance Instructions

Keys
Keys
Location
Additional Instructions

Doors
Door Code
Garage Door Code
Instructions

Alarm
Alarm Codes
Smart System Codes

Mail
Mailbox Key
Mailbox Code
Mailbox Location

Community
Community Center Code
Clubhouse Code
Common Areas Code

Service and Systems
Make note of any service
providers
Systems or technology attached
to the property

Utilities
Water
Internet
Gas
Cable TV
Sewer / Septic
Electricity
Trash

Home Owners Association
Name of HOA
President or Manager
Email or Phone
HOA Fee
HOA Fee Due

Note: It is important to have all utilities transferred at closing to ensure a smooth transition for the new homeowner. Providing a utility sheet for the home, detailing the service providers, account information, and contact numbers, can be extremely useful for the transfer of the property. This document can help the new homeowner easily set up and manage their utility services without any hassle. *This process will vary by location*.

Water Internet
Gas Cable TV
Sewer
Septic
Electricity
Trash

CREATE A BUYER / SELLER MOVING CHECKLIST

Government Services
Post Office
Schools
Library
State Licensing

Subscriptions | Deliveries
Amazon
Ebay
Newspapers
Magazines

Insurance Companies
Home or Renters
Health
Accidental
Life
Auto

Miscellaneous
Hairstylist | Spa Services
Health and Fitness Club
House of Worship
Groups or Clubs

Utilities | or Attach Utilities Sheet
Electricity
Gas
Water
Telephone
Internet
Cable

Personal | Professional Services
Doctor
Pharmacy
Dentist
Attorney
Broker
Accountant

Business Accounts
Bank Accounts
Credit Cards
Finance Companies
Local Store Accounts
Business Phone | Cell Phone

EXEMPLARY SERVICE

MODULE 1 | SECTION 8
Conclusion

CREATE THE ULTIMATE EXPERIENCE...

THE DETAILS MATTER! Regardless of what you are currently doing to service your clients and partners, or what you choose to add to your service plan, always keep documentation! Creating a system of service built into every immediate and future moment for clients, partners, and connections, allows you to scale quickly while also maintaining your standards and service at the highest level.

Work to complete, source, and fill as much of this piece as possible. How real estate agents service their clients is what truly sets them apart in the industry, and creates a memorable experience.

ASK YOURSELF...

- What branded service templates do you currently have?

- What branded service templates will you create?

- How will you communicate steps and instructions throughout the transaction?

- What extra services or experiences will you add to your business that will cater to your clients in a unique way?

- How do you personally create the ultimate client experience?

COMPREHENSIVE WRAP UP
MODULE 1 | SECTIONS 1-8
Conclusion

COLLECT YOR PIECES...
Module 1
Section 1-8

This comprehensive guide outlines the core operations, processes, and procedures of your real estate business. It includes information on administrative tasks, financial management, marketing strategies, client communication protocols, and other essential aspects of running your business. A well-documented business operations manual ensures consistency, efficiency, and scalability as you expand your business. By thoroughly documenting your process, vision, and expectations for every piece, you can easily identify when or where you may need adjustments or clarification of connections as you grow your business and gain partners. Clear direction, education, and access to materials provides a pathway for success.

MODULE 1
Universal Real Estate Agent
Operations Manual | Business
Operations Manual

Step 1
Creating Your Foundation / Business Information
Step 2
Company Culture and Connections
Step 3
Marketing
Step 4
Documents | Coordination
Step 5
Customer Relationship Management
Step 6
Social Media and Technology
Step 7
Partner Possibilities
Step 8
Exemplary Service

UNIVERSAL LAW OF GENDER:

BALANCING MASCULINE AND FEMININE ENERGIES, SUCH AS ASSERTIVENESS AND EMPATHY, IS CRUCIAL IN REAL ESTATE. THIS BALANCE ENABLES YOU TO CONNECT DEEPLY WITH CLIENTS, UNDERSTANDING THEIR NEEDS WHILE CONFIDENTLY DRIVING YOUR BUSINESS FORWARD. BY INTEGRATING THESE ENERGIES, YOU CREATE A HARMONIOUS APPROACH THAT FOSTERS STRONG CLIENT RELATIONSHIPS AND BUSINESS GROWTH.

COLLECT YOUR PIECES AND CREATE YOUR AGENT MANUALS

MODULE 2-3
Introduction

A listing agent and a buyers agent play distinct roles in a real estate transaction, representing different parties and responsibilities, sometimes working as both. Identify which role you will play if any, and clarify how you and/or your agents will conduct business on both sides of the transaction. Agents will need to conduct business according to all national, state, and local regulations regarding agency, adding any additional necessary steps to your process for compliance.

Here are the major differences between the two roles:

LISTING AGENT:
1. Represents sellers in the sale of their property.
2. Markets and promotes the property to attract potential buyers.
3. Conducts property valuations and determines listing prices.
4. Coordinates property showings and open houses.
5. Negotiates offers on behalf of the seller.
6. Facilitates the closing process and ensures all paperwork is completed accurately.

BUYER'S AGENT:
1. Represents buyers in their search for a property.
2. Assists buyers in finding suitable properties that meet their criteria.
3. Provides guidance on market trends, property values, and neighborhoods.
4. Coordinates property showings and accompanies buyers to view properties.
5. Helps buyers prepare competitive offers and negotiates on their behalf.
6. Guides buyers through the closing process and ensures a smooth transaction.

Creating an agent manual that is functional, educational, user-friendly, engaging, and easily accessible requires careful planning and attention to detail. Here are some key steps and considerations to keep in mind:

1.Define the Purpose and Scope of the Manual: Clearly outline the objectives of the manual and the specific topics it will cover. Consider the needs and skill levels of the agents who will be using the manual.

2.Organize the Content Logically: Divide the manual into sections or chapters that are easy to navigate and follow. Use headings, subheadings, and bullet points to break up the text and make it digestible.

3.Include Relevant Information: Ensure that the manual contains accurate and current information that is relevant to the agents' roles and responsibilities. Regularly update the manual to reflect any changes or updates.

4.Use a Variety of Formats: Incorporate text, images, diagrams, charts, and other visual elements to make the manual more engaging and easier to understand. Consider using infographics, videos, or interactive elements to enhance the learning experience.

5.Provide Clear Instructions and Guidelines: Clearly explain procedures, protocols, and best practices in a step-by-step manner. Use examples, case studies, and real-life scenarios to illustrate key concepts and principles.

6.Make it Interactive and Engaging: Include quizzes, exercises, and interactive elements to encourage active learning and retention of information. Consider incorporating gamification elements to make the manual more fun and engaging.

7.Ensure Accessibility and Usability: Design the manual with a user-friendly layout, clear navigation, and a searchable index or table of contents. Make sure the manual is available in both digital and print formats, and consider creating a mobile-friendly version for agents on the go.

8.Solicit Feedback for Updates: Encourage agents to provide feedback on the manual and make revisions based on their suggestions. Regularly review and update the manual to ensure it remains relevant and useful to agents.

By following these steps and considerations, you can create an agent manual that is functional, educational, user-friendly, engaging, and easily accessible, helping to support the ongoing training and development of your business.

1.Details of Creating a Manual:

-Define the purpose and scope of the manual: Clearly outline the objectives, topics, and information that will be covered in the manual.

-Organize the content logically: Divide the manual into sections or chapters that are easy to navigate and follow.

-Include relevant and up-to-date information: Ensure that the manual contains accurate and current information that is relevant to the roles and responsibilities of real estate agents.

-Use a variety of formats: Incorporate text, images, diagrams, charts, and other visual elements to make the manual more engaging and easier to understand.

-Provide clear instructions and guidelines: Clearly explain procedures, protocols, best practices, and examples in a step-by-step manner.

2.Importance of Creating a Manual:

-Consistency: A company manual helps ensure that all agents are following the same processes and procedures, leading to consistent service delivery and customer experience.

-Effciency: Having a manual in place streamlines operations, reduces errors, and saves time by providing agents with a reference guide for their daily tasks.

-Professionalism: A well-crafted manual reflects the professionalism of the company and instills confidence in clients, partners, and stakeholders.

-Training and development: The manual serves as a valuable tool for onboarding new agents, providing them with the necessary information and resources to succeed in their roles.

-Compliance: A manual helps ensure that agents are aware of and adhere to company policies, legal requirements, and industry regulations.

3.Making the Manual Functional, Educational, User-Friendly, Engaging, and Easily Accessible:

-Functional: Ensure that the manual serves its intended purpose by providing practical information and guidance for agents.

-Educational: Offer valuable insights, tips, and resources that enhance agents' knowledge and skills in the real estate industry.

-User-friendly: Design the manual with a clear layout, easy navigation, and a searchable index or table of contents for quick reference.

-Engaging: Use a variety of formats, visuals, and interactive elements to make the manual interesting and engaging for agents.

-Easily accessible: Make the manual available in both digital and print formats, and consider creating a mobile-friendly version for agents on the go. Provide easy access to the manual through a centralized platform or intranet for quick reference.

Publishing your company agent manual with the best possible options for easy access involves several steps to ensure that the company agent process is readily available and accessible to all agents.

Here is a step-by-step guide:

STEP 1: Finalize the Content - Ensure that the manual is complete, up-to-date, and contains all the necessary information for agents to perform their roles effectively.

STEP 2: Choose a Publishing Format - Decide on the format in which you want to publish the manual. Options include digital formats (PDF, eBook, online document) and print formats (hard copy, spiral-bound).

STEP 3: Design and Layout - Design the layout of the manual to be visually appealing and easy to navigate. Include a table of contents, headings, subheadings, and clear formatting for a user-friendly experience.

STEP 4: Consider Online Platforms - Explore online platforms such as company intranet, cloud storage services, or document management systems to host the manual for easy access.

STEP 5: Digital Publishing - If publishing in a digital format, convert the manual into a PDF or eBook file. Ensure compatibility with various devices and consider adding interactive elements for engagement.

STEP 6: Print Publishing - If publishing in a print format, work with a professional printing service to produce high-quality hard copies. Consider options like spiral binding for easy reference and durability.

STEP 7: Distribute the Manual - Distribute the manual to all agents through email, company intranet, or physical copies. Provide clear instructions on how to access and use the manual effectively.

STEP 8: Training and Orientation - Conduct training sessions or orientations for agents to introduce the manual, explain its contents, and demonstrate how to navigate and utilize the information effectively.

STEP 9: **Regular Updates** - Establish a process for regular updates and revisions to keep the manual current and relevant. Notify agents of any changes and provide access to updated versions.

By following these steps and utilizing digital and print publishing options, you can publish your company agent manual with the best possible options for easy access, ensuring that agents have the necessary resources at their fingertips to succeed.

A goal is a *desired outcome or objective* that a person or organization aims to achieve within a specific timeframe. In the context of broker or realtor, the primary goal should always be aligned with that of their clients. This means that the real estate agent's focus should be on understanding and *fulfilling* the needs, preferences, and objectives of their clients when it comes to buying or selling a property. By defining and prioritizing the client's goals, real estate agents can work diligently and effectively towards achieving those goals on behalf of their clients.

Honesty and integrity are fundamental values in the real estate industry, as they form the basis of *trust and credibility* in all professional relationships. Real estate transactions involve significant financial and emotional investments, and clients rely on their agents to provide accurate information, guidance, and representation throughout the process. By upholding honesty and integrity in all dealings, real estate agents can build strong, long-lasting relationships with their clients and partners, earning their respect and loyalty.

Clients and partners appreciate honesty because it fosters transparency, reliability, and trust in the real estate agent-client relationship. When clients know that their agent is acting in their best interests, providing truthful information, and offering sound advice, they feel confident and reassured in their decisions. By prioritizing honesty and integrity in their interactions, real estate agents can differentiate themselves in a competitive market and establish a reputation for professionalism and ethical conduct.

In the world of real estate, it is crucial for brokers and realtors to *prioritize* the goals and needs of their clients above all else. The primary objective should always be to support and guide clients towards achieving their desired outcomes, whether it be buying their dream home, selling a property for the best price, or investing in real estate. Real estate agents should act as trusted advisors, listening to their clients' preferences, concerns, and objectives, and working diligently to align their efforts with those goals. Leading a client in a direction that does not align with their goals or preferences can result in dissatisfaction, mistrust, and ultimately, a failed transaction.

By focusing on supporting the clients goals and *working collaboratively* towards achieving them, real estate agents can build strong, long-lasting relationships with their clients and earn their trust and loyalty. Honesty, transparency, and integrity are essential qualities that real estate agents should embody in their interactions with clients. By prioritizing the client's goals and needs above all else, real estate agents can establish themselves as reliable and trustworthy professionals, fostering positive relationships and successful outcomes. By acting from service, not sales, agents can create authentic relationships, foster a healthy leadership mindset, and grow a reputable business within their local community.

COLLECT YOUR PIECES AND CREATE YOUR AGENT MANUALS

MODULE 2-3 | Conclusion

The key difference between a listing agent and a buying agent lies in their representation of either the seller or the buyer in a real estate transaction. Each plays a crucial role in helping their clients achieve their real estate goals and navigate the complexities of buying or selling a property. However, the process of the transaction will have different procedures for each defining moment.

AGENT MANUALS STEP BY STEP:

Introduction | Lead Sheet

Documents | Phase 1-4
Buyer or Sellers Documents |
Process and Compliance

Steps 1-12
Transaction Side |
Buyer or Sellers Agent

Agent-Step By Step: Steps 1-12
Buyer or Sellers Agent |
Process + Documents

Communicate:
Key Communication Opportunities
Scripts |
Email Templates [Communication]

ASK YOURSELF...

What
- What is the task - What additional steps or tasks will be needed?

Who
- Roles or responsibilities - Attach Links and Communication [Agent to Contact] [Insert Contact Info]

When
- When will parties involved need to perform the task, or their portion of the task?

Where
- Where to find documents, items, or access points to complete the task? [Attach Links]

How
- Workflow, Process, Timing, Compliance [Attach Links, or Access Information]

UREA **SELLERS**
AGENT MANUAL

MODULE 2
SECTIONS 1-5

02.

- CREATE YOUR SELLER LEAD SHEETS | INTRODUCTION
- SELLER DOCUMENTS | [EXAMPLE] PROCESS AND COMPLIANCE: DOCUMENTS | PHASE 1-4
- TRANSACTION SIDE | [EXAMPLE] SELLERS AGENT: STEPS 1-12
- STEP BY STEP | [EXAMPLE] SELLERS AGENT / PROCESS + DOCUMENTS STEPS 1-12
- SELLERS KEY COMMUNICATION OPPORTUNITIES

UNIVERSAL REAL ESTATE AGENT SELLERS AGENT MANUAL

MODULE 2 | SECTIONS 1-5
Introduction

The role of a Listing Agent in real estate involves various responsibilities and tasks to effectively market and sell a property. Here is a step-by-step agent process with detailed guidelines to develop each stage of your business or company process.

Represents Sellers: A listing agent works on behalf of the seller to market and sell their property. They help the seller determine the listing price, prepare the property for sale, and create marketing materials to attract potential buyers.

Market Expertise: Listing agents have in-depth knowledge of the local real estate market, trends, and pricing strategies. They use this expertise to advise sellers on how to maximize the value of their property and attract qualified buyers.

Property Promotion: Listing agents are responsible for promoting the property through various channels, such as online listings, open houses, and networking with other real estate Professionals. They aim to generate interest and secure offers from potential buyers.

Negotiation: Listing agents negotiate on behalf of the seller to secure the best possible price and terms for the sale of the property. They handle offers, counter offers, and any negotiations that arise during the transaction process.

Closing Process: Listing agents guide sellers through the closing process, ensuring that all necessary paperwork is completed, and the transaction is finalized smoothly.

SELLER LEAD SHEET
SELLERS DISCLOSURE | AGENCY DISCLOSURE:
Introduction / Flow
Seller Lead Sheets: Seller lead sheets are essential tools for capturing and organizing information about potential sellers, including their contact details, property details, and timeline.
- These sheets help agents track and follow up with leads effectively, tailor their services to meet individual needs, and provide personalized assistance throughout the selling process.

MODULE 2
UNIVERSAL REAL ESTATE AGENT OPERATIONS MANUAL
SELLERS AGENT MANUAL STEPS 1-5

STEP 1	**SELLERS DISCLOSURE	AGENCY DISCLOSURE: INTRODUCTION FLOW - STEPS 1-10**
STEP 2	**SELLERS DOCUMENTS	PROCESS AND COMPLIANCE: DOCUMENTS	PHASE 1-4**
STEP 3	**TRANSACTION SIDE	SELLERS AGENT: STEPS 1-12**
STEP 4	**STEP BY STEP: SELLERS AGENT: PROCESS + DOCUMENTS - STEPS 1-12**
STEP 5	**STEP BY STEP: SELLERS AGENT	KEY COMMUNICATION OPPORTUNITIES: COMMUNICATION - STEPS 1-8**

SELLER LEAD SHEET

1. **Introduction and Background Information:** Introduce yourself and your role as a listing agent. Present any agency disclosures or legally required information. Ask for the potential's name, contact information, and property address. Inquire about the client's motivation for selling the property and their desired timeline for listing and selling.
2. **Property Details:** Gather information about the property, including the type (single-family home, condo, etc.), number of bedrooms and bathrooms, square footage, and any features or upgrades. Ask about the property's age, condition, and any recent renovations or improvements.
3. **Pricing Strategy:** Discuss the client's expectations for the listing price and inquire about their desired outcome in terms of selling price. Provide the client with a comparative market analysis to help determine the property's market value and recommend a competitive listing price at the listing appointment.
4. **Marketing Plan and Strategies:** Explain your marketing plan for the client's property, including online listings, open houses, and targeted advertising. Discuss any staging or photography services you offer to showcase the property effectively and attract potential buyers.
5. **Commission and Fees:** Review your commission rate and any additional fees associated with listing the property. Discuss the client's budget and expectations in terms of commission and fees.
6. **Communication and Updates:** Explain your communication style and how often the client can expect updates on the listing process. Inquire about the client's preferred method of communication, such as phone calls, emails, or text messages.
7. **Listing Agreement and Terms:** Discuss the listing agreement and any terms or conditions the client should be aware of before signing. Explain the length of the listing agreement and any options for canceling or extending it.
8. **Additional Services and Resources:** Offer any additional services you provide, such as home staging, virtual tours, or relocation assistance. Discuss your network of professionals, such as photographers, contractors, or inspectors, that can help prepare the property for listing.
9. **Next Steps and Follow-Up / Listing Presentation:** Summarize the information discussed during the meeting and confirm the next steps in the listing process. Schedule a follow-up meeting or property visit to further discuss the listing details and sign the agreement if the client is ready.
10. **Closing and Thank You:** Thank the potential client for considering you as their listing agent and express your enthusiasm for working with them. Provide your contact information and encourage the client to reach out with any further questions or concerns.

SELLERS DOCUMENTS | PHASE 1-4 | SYSTEM | EXAMPLE

Organize your documents into 4 phases. Introduction / Listing Presentation, New Listing, Listing Under Contract, and Listing Closed. Add the following details to each phase for clarity and compliance:

•Required Documents
•Compliance
•Requirements or Standards
•Time Frame for Submission
•Additional Details

PHASE 1 | Introduction: Any Compliance
Within: [Time Frame] [Example Documents Below]
First Introduction
Seller Presentation Guide
Local Stats
Agency or Firm Presentation Disclosures

PHASE 2 / New Listing: Submit all Documents for Compliance
Within: [Time Frame] [Example Documents Below]
Listing Agency Agreement
Agency Disclosures | Compliance
Property Card
Deed
Tax Bill
Lead Based Paint Disclosure (LBP)
Property Disclosure
Local or Regional Disclosures

PHASE 3 / Listing Under Contract: Submit all Documents for Compliance
Within: [Time Frame] [Example Documents Below]
Complete Contract
Complete Disclosures
Amendments or Requests

PHASE 4 / Listing Closed: Submit all Documents for Compliance
Within: [Time Frame] [Example Documents Below]
Seller Settlement Statement / If Required
Additional Office Documents
Additional Compliance

SELLERS AGENT STEP BY STEP
STEPS 1-12 [EXAMPLE]

Step 1: Sellers / Listing Agent - Specific Documents
Sellers Transaction : Checklist Steps 1-12 | Sellers Documents / Phase 1-4

Step 2: Sellers / Listing Agent - Property Research | Documents
Prepare CMA

Step 3: Sellers / Listing Agent - Seller's Presentation
[Complete Presentation Checklist]

Step 4: Sellers / Listing Agent - Attend the Listing Presentation

Step 5: Sellers / Listing Agent - New Listing - Marketing Plan Ready
[Attach plan]

Step 6: Sellers / Listing Agent - Enter the Property into the Multiple Listing Service
(MLS) [Attach Local MLS Link]

Step 7: Sellers / Listing Agent - Get Ready to Go Live on the Market

Step 8: Sellers / Listing Agent - MLS Active Listing: [Attach Local MLS Link]
Change Status / Active

Step 9: Sellers / Listing Agent - Under Contract: [Attach Local MLS Link]
Change Status / Under Contract

Step 10: Sellers / Listing Agent - Home Inspections - During /After

Step 11: Sellers / Listing Agent - Closing Day: [Attach Local MLS Link]
Change Status / Closed

Step 12: Sellers / Listing Agent - Celebrate Your Sellers Closing

SELLERS AGENT STEP BY STEP

PROCESS + DOCUMENTS | STEPS 1-4 [EXAMPLE]

1. Agent Specific Documents Needed | Sellers Transaction :
Sellers Checklist : Steps 1-12 | Sellers Documents : Phase 1-4

- Sellers Checklist : Steps 1-12
- Property disclosure forms.
- Seller's property questionnaire.
- Any relevant property documents (deeds, surveys, etc.).
- Additional documents may include HOA documents, inspection reports, and repair estimates.
- Documents checklist for a listing transaction should include all necessary paperwork, contracts, and disclosures required by national, state, and local regulations.

2. Sellers | Listing Agent - Property Research | Documents
Prepare CMA:

- Conduct thorough property research, including gathering information on the property's history, ownership, and any relevant documents.
- Source online links to local or state documents such as property tax records, zoning regulations, and title information.
- Utilize company systems or databases to access listing documents, property data, market trends, and comparable sales.

3. Sellers | Listing Agent - Seller's Presentation [Presentation Checklist]

- Prepare a comprehensive seller's presentation that includes market analysis reports, marketing strategies, and a detailed plan to sell the property.
- Provide a seller's guide outlining the selling process, timelines, and expectations.
- Include any specific documents related to your firm's services, marketing materials, and listing agreements.

4. Sellers | Listing Agent - Attend Listing Presentation

- Meet with the seller to discuss the listing agreement, pricing strategy, and marketing plan Sign necessary documents, including the listing agreement, seller disclosures, and any additional paperwork required.
- Begin assisting the seller to prepare the property for listing, which may involve staging, repairs, or improvements.
- Schedule professional property marketing vendors such as photographers, videographers, and measurement specialist.

SELLERS AGENT STEP BY STEP
PROCESS + DOCUMENTS | STEPS 5-8 [EXAMPLE]

5. Sellers | Listing Agent - New Listing | Marketing Plan Ready
[Attach plan]
- Develop a comprehensive marketing plan to maximize the property's exposure and attract potential buyers.
- Utilize various marketing channels such as online listings, social media, print advertising, and open houses.
- Highlight the property's features, amenities, and value proposition to appeal to a wide range of buyers.
- Plan: Market property according to your local rules, laws, regulations, and sellers agreements.

6. Sellers | Listing Agent - MLS Entry
Multiple Listing Service (MLS): [Attach Local MLS Link]
- Input accurate and detailed information about the property into the MLS system.
- Attach all relevant documents, photos, and virtual tours to enhance the listing's visibility and appeal
- Ensure that the listing complies with MLS rules and regulations.
- Plan: Market property according to your local rules, laws, regulations, and sellers agreements.

7. Sellers | Listing Agent - Get Ready | Market Live Listing
- Adhere to local company, municipality, and state regulations when marketing the listing.
- Ensure that all marketing materials and advertisements are compliant with fair housing laws and ethical guidelines.
- Monitor and track the listing's performance and adjust marketing strategies as needed.

8. Sellers | Listing Agent - MLS Active Listing
[Attach Local MLS Link]
- Change Status / Active
- Monitor the listing's activity, showings, and feedback from potential buyers.
- Communicate with agents and interested parties promptly to answer questions and provide additional information.
- Negotiate offers on behalf of the seller and guide them through the negotiation process.

SELLERS AGENT STEP BY STEP

PROCESS + DOCUMENTS | STEPS 9-12 [EXAMPLE]

9. Sellers | Listing Agent - Under Contract
- [Attach Local MLS Link] Change Status / Under Contract
- Deliver any necessary contract documents accordingly to the appropriate parties. [List: Documents / Parties]
- Maintain open and clear communication with the seller to keep the transaction on track.
- Coordinate inspections, appraisals, and any necessary repairs or contingencies.
- Ensure all parties are meeting deadlines and fulfilling their obligation.
- Attach your under contract marketing plan.

10. Sellers | Listing Agent - Home Inspections | During /After
- Have the seller prepare for the inspections.
- Prepare for the closing process by negotiating any requests or repair negotiations.
- Prepare or review final documents for closing according to your company and legal guidelines, including the settlement statement, deed, and any other required paperwork.
- Notify the seller of any additional documents, information, codes, or services needed for closing Submit any additional documents for compliance or closing.
- Facilitate / Approve / Confirm: buyer walkthrough if necessary.

11. Sellers | Listing Agent - Closing Day | [Attach Local MLS Link]
- Change Status / Closed
- Help ensure that the settlement of the transaction is carried out according to the terms of the contract.
- Coordinate with the title company, escrow agent, and other parties involved in the closing process.
- Provide support and assistance to the seller throughout the closing process. Help facilitate transfer of any additional property information.
- Celebrate with all parties!

12. Sellers | Listing Agent - Celebrate Your Sellers Closing
- Celebrate the successful closing with the seller and express gratitude for their business.
- Market the closed listing through social media, email campaigns, and post-closing follow-up.
- Request testimonials or referrals from satisfied sellers to build your reputation and attract future clients.
- Attach your post closing marketing plan.

SELLERS AGENT MANUAL

MODULE 2 | SECTIONS 1-5
Conclusion

CREATE YOUR SELLERS KEY COMMUNICATION OPPORTUNITIES :

Key Communication Opportunity 1:
Listing Agreement Signed:
Key Communication Opportunity 2:
Photography Session:
Key Communication Opportunity 3:
Listing Goes Live:
Key Communication Opportunity 4:
Open House:
Key Communication Opportunity 5:
Offer Received:
Key Communication Opportunity 6:
Offer Accepted:
Key Communication Opportunity 7:
Home Inspection:
Key Communication Opportunity 8:
Closing Day:

ASK YOURSELF...

If sellers agents develop a detailed step-by-step manual for each phase of their sellers process, they can enhance confidence in their methods and provide clarity for all involved.

Create your lead sheet: What will you add to your buyer lead sheet? Does your business have a niche?

Define your model: Clarify the level of education, or instruction you will add. What are the steps you will use for your sellers agent process?

Documents: List the required documents for your sellers transaction. Add any additional local disclosures or firm documents. Have you listed your documents in phases according to your process?

Process: Define the workflow for each step of your sellers agent process. Where will you store scripts, lead sheets, your manuals, marketing information, and any additional templates or materials?

UNIVERSAL LAW OF PERPETUAL TRANSMUTATION OF ENERGY:

ENERGY IS CONSTANTLY CHANGING FORMS, AND IN REAL
ESTATE, CHANNELING YOUR PASSION AND CREATIVITY
CAN TRANSFORM IDEAS INTO IMPACTFUL SERVICES.
BY EMBRACING CHANGE AND INNOVATION,
YOU CAN DEVELOP NEW STRATEGIES AND
OFFERINGS THAT EFFECTIVELY SERVE
YOUR CLIENTS, ENSURING YOUR
BUSINESS REMAINS DYNAMIC
AND COMPETITIVE.

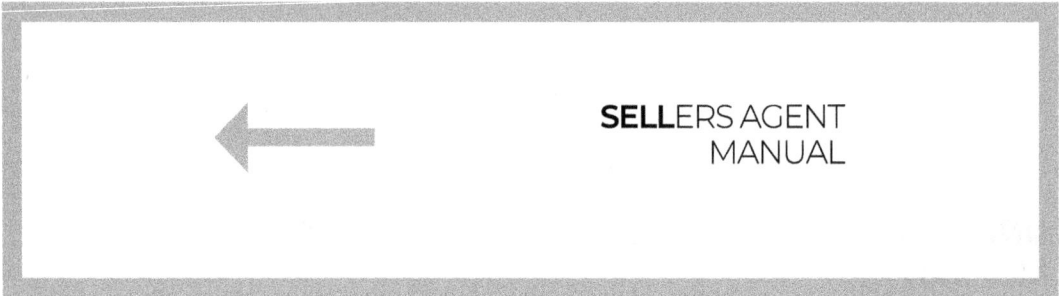

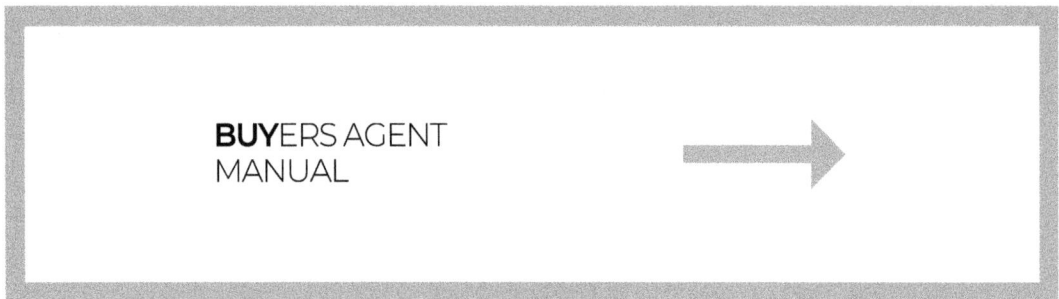

UREA **BUYERS**
AGENT MANUAL

MODULE 3
SECTIONS 1-5

03.

- CREATE YOUR BUYER LEAD SHEETS | INTRODUCTION
- BUYER DOCUMENTS | [EXAMPLE] PROCESS AND COMPLIANCE: DOCUMENTS | PHASE 1-4
- TRANSACTION SIDE | [EXAMPLE] BUYERS AGENT | STEPS 1-12
- STEP BY STEP| [EXAMPLE] BUYERS AGENT / PROCESS + DOCUMENTS: STEPS 1-12
- BUYERS COMMUNICATION OPPORTUNITIES

UNIVERSAL REAL ESTATE AGENT
BUYERS AGENT MANUAL

MODULE 3 | SECTIONS 1-5
Introduction

The role of a buyer's agent in real estate involves various responsibilities and tasks to effectively complete a buyer's transaction. Here is a step-by-step buyer's agent process with detailed guidelines for each stage.

Buyers Agent: A buying agent works on behalf of the buyer to help them find and purchase a property that meets their needs and budget. They assist buyers in identifying suitable properties, making offers, and navigating the purchase process.

Buyer Representation: Buying agents advocate for the buyer's best interests throughout the transaction, providing guidance, advice, and support to help them make informed decisions.

Property Search: Buying agents help buyers search for properties that match their criteria, schedule showings, and provide information on market conditions, property values, and neighborhood amenities.

Offer Preparation: Buying agents assist buyers in preparing and submitting offers on properties, including negotiating terms, contingencies, and price. They work to secure the best possible deal for the buyer.

Closing Process: Buying agents guide buyers through the closing process, coordinating with lenders, inspectors, title companies, and other parties involved in the transaction. They ensure that all necessary steps are taken to complete the purchase successfully.

BUYER LEAD SHEET
BUYERS DISCLOSURE | AGENCY DISCLOSURE:
Introduction / Flow
Buyer Lead Sheets: - Buyer lead sheets are essential tools for capturing and organizing information about potential buyers, including their contact details, preferences, budget, and timeline.
- These sheets help agents track and follow up with leads effectively, tailor their services to meet individual needs, and provide personalized assistance throughout the buying process.

MODULE 3
UNIVERSAL REAL ESTATE AGENT OPERATIONS MANUAL
BUYERS AGENT MANUAL STEPS 1-5

STEP 1	**BUYERS DISCLOSURE	AGENCY DISCLOSURE:** **INTRODUCTION FLOW - STEPS 1-10**
STEP 2	**BUYERS DOCUMENTS	PROCESS AND COMPLIANCE:** **DOCUMENTS	PHASE 1-4**
STEP 3	**TRANSACTION SIDE	BUYERS AGENT:** **STEPS 1-12**
STEP 4	**STEP BY STEP: BUYERS AGENT:** **PROCESS + DOCUMENTS - STEPS 1-12**
STEP 5	**STEP BY STEP: BUYERS AGENT	COMMUNICATION** **OPPORTUNITIES : COMMUNICATION - STEPS 1-8**

BUYER LEAD SHEET

1. **Introduction:** Introduce yourself and your role as a real estate agent. - Ask for the buyer's name and contact information. Present any agency disclosures or legally required information

2. **Buyer's Needs:** Inquire about the buyer's specific needs in terms of property type (house, condo, townhouse), number of bedrooms and bathrooms, desired location, budget, and any specific features they are looking for. Ask about their timeline for purchasing a property.

3. **Buyer's Wants:** Explore the buyer's preferences and wants, such as style of home (modern, traditional, etc.), amenities (pool, gym, etc.), and any specific neighborhood or school district preferences. Inquire about any must-have features or deal-breakers.

4. **Buyer's Wishes:** Discuss the buyer's ideal scenario, including any additional features or amenities they would like to have but are not essential. Ask about any long-term goals or considerations that may impact their decision.

5. **Property Preferences:** Inquire about the buyer's preferred property size, layout, and design. Ask about their willingness to consider properties that may need some renovation or updates.

6. **Financing:** Discuss the buyer's financing options, including pre-approval status and a comfortable price range to work in. Inquire about their comfort level with the down payment amount and monthly mortgage payments.

7. **Viewing Preferences:** Ask about the buyer's availability for property viewings and any specific scheduling preferences. Inquire about their preferred method of communication for updates on new listings and property showings.

8. **Follow-Up:** Summarize the information gathered during the call and confirm the next steps. Schedule a follow-up meeting or property tour based on the buyer's availability and preferences.

9. **Additional Questions:** Ask if the buyer has any questions or concerns that have not been addressed. Offer to start a local home search portal and provide additional information or resources to help them in their home search.

10. **Closing:** Thank the buyer for their time and interest in working with you as their agent. Reiterate your commitment to helping them find their dream home and provide your contact information.

BUYERS DOCUMENTS | PHASE 1-4 | SYSTEM

Organize your documents into four phases. Introduction, New Buyer, Buyer Under Contract, and Buyer Closed. Add the following details to each phase for clarity and compliance:

• Required Documents
• Compliance
• Requirements or Standards
• Time Frame for Submission
• Additional Details

PHASE 1 | Introduction: Any Compliance
Within: [Time Frame] [Example Documents Below]
Buyer Presentation Guide / Disclosure
Pre-Qualification
Agency or Company Compliance Disclosures
Sample Documents

PHASE 2 / New Buyer: Submit all Documents for Compliance
Within: [Time Frame] [Example Documents Below]
Buyer Agency (BAA) Agreements
Title Company Affiliations
Other Affiliation Disclosures
Agency Disclosures

PHASE 3 / Buyer Under Contract: Submit all Documents for Compliance
Within: [Time Frame] [Example Documents Below]
Contract / Property Information
Lead Based Paint Disclosure (LBP)
Property Disclosures
Local or Regional Disclosures

PHASE 4 / Buyer Closed: Submit all Documents for Compliance
Within: [Time Frame] [Example Documents Below]
Buyer Settlement Statement If Required
Additional Required Office Documents
Additional Compliance Steps

BUYERS AGENT STEP BY STEP

STEPS 1-12 [EXAMPLE]

Step 1: Buyers Agent | Specific Documents Needed
Buyers Transaction : Checklist Steps 1-12 | Buyers Documents / Phase 1-4

Step 2: Buyers Agent | Specific Documents
Checklist : Buyers Presentation / Preparation

Step 3: Buyers Agent | Buyer's Presentation
[Complete Presentation Checklist | Attend Presentation]

Step 4: Buyers Agent | Setting Up Buyer's Property Search
[Attach Local MLS Link]

Step 5: Buyers Agent | Scheduling Property Showings
[Attach Local MLS Link] [Attach Showing Platform Instructions]

Step 6: Buyers Agent | Follow NAR Guidelines for Showing a Home
[Attach] Guidelines and Showing Instructions

Step 7: Buyers Agent | Offer to Purchase
Submit Offer | Offer Accepted

Step 8: Buyers Agent | Under Contract
Buyers Inspections: [Attach Local Vendor List]

Step 9: Buyers Agent | Property Inspections
[Communicate | All Parties]

Step 10: Buyers Agent | Prepare for Closing

Step 11: Buyers Agent | Buyer Closing Day

Step 12: Buyers Agent | Celebrate Buyers Closing

BUYERS AGENT STEP BY STEP

PROCESS + DOCUMENTS | STEPS 1-4 [EXAMPLE]

1. Buyers Agent | Specific Documents Needed

Buyers Transaction : Checklist | Buyers Documents / Phase 1-4

[platforms / Links]

- Buyer representation agreement
- Purchase agreement
- Pre-approval letter Proof of funds
- Identification documents
- Property disclosure forms
- Inspection reports
- Appraisal report
- Title documents
- Loan documents
- Documents checklist for a buyers transaction should include all necessary paperwork, contracts, and disclosures required by national, state, and local regulations

2. Buyers Agent | Specific Documents

Checklist for your buyers presentation | Preparation

- Buyer representation agreement
- Agency documents or disclosures
- Company disclosures Specific documents / disclosures / or sample documents

3. Buyers Agent | Attend Buyer's Presentation [Presentation Checklist]:

- Buyer's guide
- Market analysis reports
- Comparative market analysis for listings of interest
- Specific documents, disclosures, or sample documents

4. Buyers Agent | Setting Up Buyer's Property Search: [Attach Local MLS Link]

- Understand buyer preferences and criteria
- Utilize MLS listings and search tools
- Set up automated property alerts
- Regularly update and refine the property search based on feedback

BUYERS AGENT STEP BY STEP

PROCESS + DOCUMENTS | STEPS 5-8 [EXAMPLE]

5. Buyers Agent | Scheduling Property Showings
- [Attach Local MLS Link] [Attach Showing platform Instructions]
- Coordinate with sellers or listing agents / MLS
- Confirm availability with buyers
- Provide property details and directions
- Allow sufficient time for each showing / Follow guidelines for showing homes

6. Buyers Agent | Follow Guidelines When Showing Property:
[Attach] Company / Personal Guidelines + Showing Instructions
- Obtain permission from the seller
- Respect the property and belongings
- Ensure safety and security during showings
- Provide accurate information to buyers
- Follow ethical and professional conduct

7. Buyers Agent | Tips And Tricks When Writing An Offer:
Submit Offer / Offer Accepted
- Conduct thorough property research, including gathering information on the property's history, ownership, and any relevant documents before submitting an offer.
- Include all necessary terms and conditions Be clear and concise in the offer
- Submit a competitive offer based on your clients wishes
- Communicate effectively with the seller or listing agent
- Attach a list of necessary documents , scripts, and steps for submitting an offer / [Attach Documents Link]
- Buyer under contract: Send to: [Complete Documents] + [Parties] / [Compliance Storage Link]

8. Buyers Agent | Under Contract - Buyers Inspection:
[Attach Local Vendor List] Schedule Inspections | Avoid Delays
- Help the buyer have inspections performed according to the contract, and in the inspection period agreed upon
- Review the inspection report thoroughly with the buyer / Address any concerns or issues with the property
- Negotiate repairs or credits if needed

BUYERS AGENT STEP BY STEP

PROCESS + DOCUMENTS | STEPS 9-12 [EXAMPLE]

9. Buyers Agent | After Property Inspections: [Communicate with all parties]
- Communicate inspection findings to the lender if required
- Provide any additional documentation or information required
- Address any appraisal issues, lender, or client concerns
- Notify parties when any required or agreed upon repairs have been completed
- Confirm with the buyer when the loan has been approved, and help them begin to prepare for closing

10. Buyers Agent | Prepare With All Parties For Closing:
- Ensure all closing documents are in order
- Coordinate with the title company and lender
- Review closing costs and fees with the buyer
- Confirm the closing date and time
- Confirm all documents are in order for company compliance
- Schedule and confirm the buyers final walkthrough

11. Buyers Agent | Buyer Closing Day:
- Help facilitate the transfer of ownership according to the contract details
- Ensure all parties are present for their scheduled closings
- Keep in close contact with the listing agent
- Help buyer review and sign closing documents as legally required
- Facilitate for the buyer to receive keys and possession of the property - According to the contract terms and conditions
- Celebrate with all parties!

12. Buyers Agent | Celebrate Your Buyers Closing:
- Celebrate the successful closing with the buyer
- Share the news on social media and with your network
- Ask for referrals and testimonials from satisfied clients
- Stay in touch with the buyer for future opportunities

BUYERS AGENT MANUAL

MODULE 3 | SECTIONS 1-5
Conclusion

CREATE YOUR BUYERS KEY COMMUNICATION OPPORTUNITIES :

Key Communication Opportunity 1:
Initial Consultation:

Key Communication Opportunity 2:
Pre-Approval:

Key Communication Opportunity 3:
Offer Accepted:

Key Communication Opportunity 4:
Home Inspection:

Key Communication Opportunity 5:
Appraisal:

Key Communication Opportunity 6:
Loan Approval:

Key Communication Opportunity 7:
Final Walkthrough:

Key Communication Opportunity 8:
Closing Day:

ASK YOURSELF...

If buyers agents develop a detailed step-by-step manual for each phase of their buyers process, they can enhance confidence in their methods and provide clarity for all involved.

Create your lead sheet: What will you add to your buyer lead sheet? Does your business have a niche?

Define your model: Clarify the level of education, or instruction you will add. What are the steps you will use for your process?

Documents: List the required documents for your buyers transaction. Add any additional local disclosures or firm documents. Have you listed your documents in phases according to your process?

Process: Define the workflow for each step of your process. Where will you store scripts, lead sheets, your manuals, marketing information, and any additional templates or materials.

UREA GAINING
PARTNERS MANUAL

MODULE 4
SECTIONS 1-5

04.

- UREA GAINING PARTNERS SYSTEM
- RECRUITING TOP TALENT
- CREATE YOUR COMPANY PARTNER GUIDE
- CREATE YOUR AGENT PARTNER GUIDE
- GAINING PARTNERS / DEFINE YOUR PROCESS
- CREATE YOUR AGENT PARTNER COMMUNICATION / CELEBRATION OPPORTUNITIES FOR RETENTION

UNIVERSAL REAL ESTATE AGENT GAINING PARTNERS MANUAL

MODULE 4 | SECTIONS 1-5
Introduction

MODULE 4
UNIVERSAL REAL ESTATE AGENT OPERATIONS MANUAL
GAINING PARTNERS MANUAL STEPS 1-5

STEP 1	PARTNER STANDARDS	TALENT REQUIREMENTS
STEP 2	GAINING PARTNERS MANUAL	SERVICE GUIDE
STEP 3	AGENT SAMPLES
STEP 4	PUBLIC PRINT MARKETING SAMPLES
STEP 5	AGENT RELATIONSHIP MANAGEMENT MATERIALS

PERSONALIZE YOUR PARTNER SYSTEM

Company Partner Guide Partner Standards | Talent Requirements: Outlines the criteria, process, and strategies for recruiting and selecting strategic partners to support your real estate business. It includes tips for identifying potential partners, evaluating their qualifications, negotiating agreements, and establishing productive working relationships according to your vision and standards.

Agent Partner Guide: Including agent presentations in your partner packet can help showcase your company's values, culture, and offerings to potential recruits. These presentations can highlight the benefits of joining your team, such as training, technology tools, and support systems, to attract top talent and set clear expectations for new agents.

Print Marketing Samples: Providing print marketing samples, such as brochures, flyers, and postcards, can give recruits a tangible representation of your company's branding and marketing efforts. This can help convey your company's professionalism, attention to detail, and commitment to quality, which can resonate with potential agents and differentiate your company from competitors.

Agent Marketing | Agent Marketing Samples: Including agent marketing samples, such as business cards, digital marketing materials, and listing presentations, can demonstrate the marketing resources and tools available to agents within your company. This can show recruits how they can effectively market themselves and their listings, attract clients, and grow their business with the support of your company's marketing resources.

Print Mail Shipping | Agent Relationship Management Materials: Providing agent relationship management materials, such as letters, email templates, and strategies for farming your sphere of influence, can help recruits understand the importance of building and maintaining client relationships in the real estate industry. These materials can offer guidance on how to nurture leads, stay in touch with past clients, and grow their network to generate referrals and repeat business.

Set Expectations

By creating a company partner guide that outlines partner standards and talent requirements, you establish a clear framework for selecting and working with partners. This guide serves as a roadmap for your team, ensuring that everyone is aligned on the criteria for choosing partners and the expectations for collaboration.

Create Confidence

Having a structured guide in place helps to create confidence within your organization as it provides a transparent standardized process for partnering with external entities. This transparency instills trust among team members, partners, and stakeholders, as they understand the criteria and rationale behind partnership decisions.

Be Consistent

Consistency is key when it comes to expanding your business and forming new partnerships. By adhering to the guidelines outlined in the partner guide, you can ensure that each new partnership aligns with your company's values, goals, and standards. This consistency not only helps to maintain the integrity of your brand but also streamlines the process of onboarding new partners and integrating them into your operations.

Maintain Standards

By creating a company partner guide that outlines partner standards, and talent requirements, you establish a solid foundation for growth and expansion. This guide fosters a culture of accountability, professionalism, and collaboration within your organization, maintaining your standards and ultimately leading to successful partnerships and sustainable business growth.

Creating a *company guide* that outlines your *partner standards and talent requirements* is essential for ensuring successful collaborations in business. This guide should include the following:

Partner Selection Criteria: This section should outline the qualities and characteristics you are looking for in a partner. This could include factors such as industry experience, reputation, financial stability, and alignment with your company values.

Standards and Expectations: Clearly define the standards and expectations you have for your partners in terms of performance, communication, and deliverables. This will help set clear guidelines for both parties and ensure that everyone is on the same page.

Talent Requirements: Identify the specific skills and expertise that you are looking for in a partner. This could include technical skills, industry knowledge, or creative abilities that are essential for the success of the partnership.

Tips for Identifying Potential Partners: Provide guidance on how to identify and approach potential partners, including networking strategies, industry events, and online research techniques.

Evaluating Qualifications: Outline a process for evaluating the qualifications of potential partners, including conducting interviews, reviewing portfolios, and checking references. This will help ensure that you are selecting partners who are capable of meeting your needs.

Negotiating Agreements: Provide tips for negotiating agreements with partners, including how to establish clear terms and conditions, define roles and responsibilities, and set expectations for timelines and deliverables.

Establishing Productive Working Relationships: Offer advice on how to establish and maintain productive working relationships with partners, including effective communication strategies, conflict resolution techniques, and regular check-ins to ensure that the partnership is on track.

By creating a *comprehensive guide* that covers these key areas, you can help ensure that your partnerships are successful, efficient, and mutually beneficial for all parties.

A *partner guide* is a valuable tool for real estate professionals as they start to build their business and attract talent to their firm, team, or business. This *comprehensive* resource serves as a guide that outlines the company's mission, vision, values, culture, benefits, and opportunities for potential partners. By presenting this information in a structured and engaging format, a partner guide can effectively showcase the unique selling points of the company and help attract top talent to join.

A partner guide also plays a crucial role in setting clear expectations for potential partners and aligning them with the business goals and objectives. It provides insight into the company's history, leadership, market positioning, and growth opportunities. This gives possible partners a comprehensive understanding of what to expect when joining the team. This *transparency* helps build trust and credibility with potential hires and ensures that they have a clear understanding of the company's values and expectations.

Clear and Concise Messaging: Clearly define your business mission, vision, and values to convey a strong brand identity. Highlight the unique selling points and benefits of joining your business to attract and engage potential agents.

Comprehensive Services Overview: Provide a detailed overview of the services and resources offered by your business, including marketing support, training programs, technology tools, and administrative assistance. Showcase success stories, testimonials, and case studies to demonstrate the effectiveness of your services.

Competitive Compensation and Incentives: Outline the commission structure, bonus programs, and incentive opportunities available to agents within your business. Clearly define the benefits package, including health insurance, retirement plans, and other perks offered to agents.

Training and Development Programs: Detail the training and mentorship programs available to new agents to support their professional growth and success. Highlight continuing education opportunities, certifications, and networking events provided by your business.

Compliance and Support: Emphasize the importance of compliance and regulatory adherence within your business to ensure agents operate ethically and legally. Provide information on the administrative support, transaction coordination, and compliance assistance offered to agents.

Technology and Marketing Tools: Showcase the technology platforms, CRM systems, and marketing tools available to agents to streamline their operations and enhance their marketing efforts. Highlight any proprietary tools or resources exclusive to your business that give agents a competitive edge.

Company Culture and Team Dynamics: Communicate the company culture, values, and team dynamics to give potential agents insight into the work environment and collaboration opportunities. Include testimonials from current agents and team members to showcase the positive work culture and camaraderie within the business.

Growth Opportunities: Outline the career advancement opportunities, leadership development programs, and pathways for growth within your business. Illustrate the potential for agents to progress in their careers, take on leadership roles, and achieve their professional goals.

A partner guide can serve as a powerful marketing tool to differentiate the company from competitors and position it as an employer or partner of choice in the real estate industry. By highlighting the company's unique culture, support systems, training programs, and career advancement opportunities, a partner guide can attract top talent who align with the company's values and vision. Overall, a well-crafted partner guide can help real estate professionals build a strong team, foster a positive company culture, and drive success and growth in their business.

STEP 1.

Partner Standards | Talent Requirements | Retention Plan For Agents:

- Criteria, process, and strategies for recruiting, selecting, and retaining strategic partners to support your real estate business.

STEP 2.

Partner Guide:

- Logo / Slogan: Culture | Company/Business mission, vision, values, beliefs, and goals
- Exemplary service options or partners
- Company branding and marketing options available / Marketing plans or partners
- Printing or shipping options or partners
- Document or compliance support
- CRM / Technology / Platforms - Leads, or leverage offered
- The benefits of partnering with your company - Added value
- Education and access to education / Coaching or training programs available
- Partnerships, ownership, ways to invest in the future
- Company commission standards

STEP 3.

Agent Marketing | Agent Presentations | Samples:

- Business cards, digital marketing materials, and listing presentations, can demonstrate the marketing resources and tools available to agents within your company.

STEP 4.

Property Presentations | Samples:

- Public Digital Marketing - Samples
- Public Print Marketing - Samples
- Brochures, flyers, and postcards, can give recruits a tangible representation of your company's branding and marketing efforts.

STEP 5.

Agent Relationship Management Materials:

- Communication
- Letters, email templates, and strategies for farming your sphere of influence, can help recruits understand the importance of building and maintaining client relationships.

GAINING PARTNERS MANUAL

MODULE 4 | SECTIONS 1-5
Conclusion

**AGENT KEY COMMUNICATION /
CELEBRATION OPPORTUNITIES:**

Agent Birthday:
Top Producer | Goal Reached
Work Anniversary |
Year 1 - Year 5 -Year 10:
Key Communication Opportunity 1:
First Sale:
Key Communication Opportunity 2:
Closing a High-Value Deal:
Key Communication Opportunity 3:
Reaching a Sales Goal:
Key Communication Opportunity 4:
Winning an Award:
Key Communication Opportunity 5:
Closing a Difficult Deal:
Key Communication Opportunity 6:
Growing Your Client Base:
Key Communication Opportunity 7:
Achieving a Certification or
Designation:
Key Communication Opportunity 8:
Achieving a Social Media Milestone:
Key Communication Opportunity 9:
Hosting a Successful Client
Appreciation Event:
**Key Communication Opportunity
10:**
Personal Growth Milestones:

ASK YOURSELF...
- **Recruiting Partners:** What criteria, process, and strategies will you use for recruiting, selecting, and retaining strategic partners to support your real estate business?
- **Partner Guide:** What makes your company stand out from the rest? What will you offer or do differently for your partners?
- **Agent Marketing:** Have you collected samples of your business cards, digital marketing materials, and listing presentations, to demonstrate the marketing resources and tools available to agents within your company?
- **Property Marketing:** Have you collected your business brochures, flyers, and postcards, to give recruits a tangible representation of your company's property branding and marketing efforts?
- **Agent Relationship Management Materials:** Have you collected letters, email templates, and strategies for farming your sphere of influence, to help recruits understand the importance of building and maintaining client relationships?
- **Retention - Agent Celebration / Opportunities:** Have you created your agent retention plan? What opportunities are available to agents?

167

UNIVERSAL LAW OF RHYTHM:

RECOGNIZING NATURAL BUSINESS CYCLES ALLOWS YOU TO ANTICIPATE DEMAND FLUCTUATIONS. BY ALIGNING YOUR STRATEGIES WITH THESE RHYTHMS, YOU CAN BETTER SERVE CLIENTS THROUGH VARIOUS MARKET CONDITIONS. THIS AWARENESS HELPS YOU ADAPT TO CHANGES, OPTIMIZE YOUR OPERATIONS, AND MAINTAIN CLIENT SATISFACTION AND BUSINESS STABILITY.

UREA **ONBOARDING** PARTNERS MANUAL

MODULE 5
SECTIONS 1-4

05.

- ONBOARDING PARTNERS MANUAL | SYSTEM INTRODUCTION
- PARTNER ONBOARDING
- VIRTUAL ONBOARDING
- SERVICE DELIVERY THROUGH TECHNOLOGY
- DEVELOPING YOUR PROCESS
- STEP BY STEP ONBOARDING PROCESS
- ONBOARDING [PHASE / STEPS 1-4] STORAGE

UNIVERSAL REAL ESTATE AGENT ONBOARDING PARTNERS MANUAL

MODULE 5 | SECTIONS 1-4
Introduction

MODULE 5
UNIVERSAL REAL ESTATE AGENT OPERATIONS MANUAL
ONBOARDING PARTNERS MANUAL STEPS 1-5

STEP 1	AGENT PARTNERED	SIGN DOCUMENTS
STEP 2	AFTER SIGNING	DURING TRANSFER
STEP 3	THE DAY OF TRANSFER	WELCOME!
STEP 4	AFTER ONBOARDING	STEPS FOR ADJUSTMENT

PHASE | STEP 1.
Introduction Agent Partnered | Sign Documents:

The onboarding process should be clearly communicated, whether it will be done in person or remotely. This ensures a smooth transition for the agent into the business, team, or firm. Sign initial documents and company contracts. Attach contracts, commission standards, partner agreements, and communication to your company onboarding partners manual.

PHASE | STEP 2.
After Signing | During Transfer :

The agent will need to complete tasks such as filling out paperwork, attending orientation sessions, training, and familiarizing themselves with the business, team, or firm's policies, procedures, and systems. Prepare listings for transfer if that is an option, and layout any necessary steps that will need to take place on the day of transfer for the business, team, firm or the agent. Notify the agent to prepare.

PHASE | STEP 3.
The Day of Transfer :

Transfer listings if that is an option, and layout any necessary steps that will need to take place for the business, team, firm, or the agent. Attach any forms, documents, communication, or steps for compliance. Attach links, or platforms to access forms or documents to transfer listings.

PHASE | STEP 4.
After Onboarding :
Create a list of items or tasks that will need to be completed, and instructions or compliance to complete. Deliver education and orientation materials in both digital and print if that is an option. Attach links and connections for any technology or platforms available to your agent partners.

When establishing an effective onboarding process, it is essential to structure it in a way that is clear and systematic. This can be achieved by organizing the process into four distinct phases or steps, each containing 3 specific sections.

SECTION 1.
Workflow

The first section will focus on outlining the rules and responsibilities that apply to both the business and the agent. This foundational framework ensures that all parties are aware of their obligations and expectations, which is critical for fostering a productive working relationship. By clearly defining roles, it minimizes confusion and sets the stage for accountability from the outset.

SECTION 2.
Communication

The second section will emphasize communication, detailing the emails or communication links relevant to each step of the onboarding process. Effective communication is vital for ensuring that all parties remain informed and engaged throughout the onboarding journey. By providing specific contact points and resources for each step, we can facilitate timely responses to questions or concerns, thereby enhancing the overall onboarding experience. This section will serve as a roadmap for communication, ensuring that agents know where to turn for assistance or further information as they navigate the onboarding process.

SECTION 3.
Documents

Finally, the third section will include essential documents or attachments that correspond with each step of the onboarding process. These documents may include training materials, policy manuals, compliance guidelines, or any other pertinent resources that support the agent's integration into the business. By providing these materials upfront, we equip new agents with the tools they need to succeed, ensuring they have access to vital information that will aid in their transition. Together, these three sections for each step creates a comprehensive onboarding framework that promotes clarity, communication, and resource accessibility, ultimately leading to a smoother and more effective onboarding experience.

The decision to onboard in person or remotely to a real estate business will depend on the specific needs and preferences of the business, team, or firm and the new agent or partner. A combination of both approaches, such as a hybrid model that includes virtual meetings and in-person training sessions, may provide the best of both worlds and ensure a successful onboarding experience for all parties involved. Clear communication, organization, and support are key to a successful onboarding process, regardless of the method chosen.

Each firm or team is responsible for onboarding staff or agents in accordance with their specific local rules and regulations. This localized approach ensures compliance with legal requirements and industry standards that may vary significantly from one jurisdiction to another. By adhering to these regulations, firms can mitigate risks and create a structured onboarding process that aligns with best practices in their respective areas. It is crucial to clarify any key trigger points throughout the onboarding process, as these milestones often indicate critical moments when specific actions or decisions need to be made. Being precise in setting up the onboarding process allows for a smoother transition for new agents, reducing the likelihood of oversight or miscommunication.

The duration and pace of the onboarding process can vary widely based on the business structure, location, and regulatory environment of the firm. All four steps of the onboarding process may occur over the span of a week, within a few days, or even all in the same day. This flexibility allows teams to tailor their onboarding approach to best meet their operational needs and the unique circumstances of each new agent. By accommodating different timelines, firms can ensure that new hires receive the necessary training and resources at a pace that suits both their learning style and the demands of the business.

Additionally, it is pertinent to detail how the transfer of agents and their listings will occur if that option is available on the day of transfer. This involves outlining the specific procedures for transitioning client listings and ensuring that all necessary documentation is completed to facilitate a seamless handover. Clear communication regarding this process is essential to maintain client relationships and uphold the integrity of the business. By providing a well-defined strategy for transferring agents and their listings, firms can enhance the onboarding experience and reinforce trust with both new hires and clients.

Remote onboarding for real estate agents can be appealing for those who need to stay anonymous when sourcing firms, as it offers privacy, flexibility, efficiency, access to a wider range of opportunities, and enhanced security.

Privacy:
Virtual onboarding allows real estate agents to maintain their anonymity during the initial stages of the hiring process. They can participate in virtual interviews, training sessions, and orientation without revealing their identity until they are ready to do so.

Flexibility:
Virtual onboarding offers flexibility in terms of scheduling and location. Real estate agents can complete training and orientation at their own pace and convenience, without the need to physically visit the company's office or meet in person.

Efficiency:
Virtual onboarding can be more efficient as it eliminates the need for travel time and expenses. Agents can quickly onboard and start working without the delays associated with in-person meetings and training sessions.

Wider Pool of Opportunities:
Virtual onboarding allows real estate agents to explore job opportunities located in different regions or countries. They can apply for positions and onboard remotely, expanding their job prospects without the need to relocate. Support staff, virtual assistants, and many of the positions powering a real estate company can now be sourced all over the country, widening your range of talented partner options.

Enhanced Security:
Virtual onboarding can provide a higher level of security and confidentiality for real estate agents who need to protect their personal information. They can securely access training materials and communicate with the company's representatives without compromising their anonymity.

Embracing technology to deliver services in the real estate industry is essential for staying competitive, efficient, and client-focused. Creating a concrete onboarding process that aligns with your vision, values, and service standards is key to establishing a strong foundation for your real estate business, and delivering exceptional experiences to your agent partners from day one.

AGENT ONBOARDING: Partnered onboarding services can help streamline the process, and create extra support for individuals, optimizing operations within the business, team, or firm. Reducing the time for training, while also ensuring confidence in partnering or transitioning from day one. The business, team, or firm will need to complete a standard step by step process to attach any and all communication.

1. In the Introduction Stage:
It is important to define the onboarding process for remote real estate agents, outlining what will happen and who will complete each task. This sets clear expectations for both the agent and the business, team, or firm when onboarding remotely.

2. When the Agent Signs to Affiliate With the Business, Team, Or Firm:
The onboarding process should be completed as communicated whenever it will be done remotely. This ensures a smooth transition for the agent into the business, team, or firm, and builds confidence.

3. During the Onboarding Process:
The agent will need to complete tasks such as filling out paperwork, attending remote orientation sessions, training, and familiarizing themselves with the business, team, or firm's policies, procedures, and systems. Organization is key.

4. Provide Support and Guidance to The Agent:
Throughout the onboarding process, assigning tasks, providing necessary resources, and ensuring that the agent has everything they need to succeed and onboard remotely at their own convenience.

5. Welcome!!
Affiliation Information: Business / Team / Firm
Orientation : Educational Materials

Creating a step-by-step onboarding process with all necessary documents, business, team, or firm agreements, pay structures, and orientation materials can greatly improve the onboarding experience for new and experienced agents. By attaching email templates and instructions for both agents and the office, a personalized system for functionality can be established, ensuring a smooth and efficient onboarding. Here are a few reasons why a step-by-step process can be extremely beneficial:

Clarity:
- A detailed step-by-step process provides clarity for new agents, outlining expectations, tasks, and timelines for each stage of onboarding. Create a checklist of items to be completed by the business, team, or firm and by the agent.

Consistency:
- A standardized onboarding process ensures that all new agents receive the same information and training, maintaining consistency in the quality of onboarding.

Efficiency:
- Having all documents, agreements, email templates, and orientation materials readily available streamlines the onboarding process, saving time for both the agents and the office. Distinguish if agents will onboard in person, remotely, or if they will have a choice of either.

Compliance:
- By including all necessary legal documents and the business, team, or firm's agreements in the onboarding process, compliance with regulations and company policies is ensured from the start.

Personalization:
- Email templates and instructions tailored to the specific needs of agents and the office create a personalized onboarding experience, fostering a positive and welcoming environment for new team members.

ONBOARDING PIECES YOU MAY NEED FOR PARTNERS / GENERAL:

- Agent information intake sheet
- License / Boards / Associations
- Ethics information
- Company contracts and addendum's
- Payment structure sheets
- Legal, financial, or tax documents
- Agent checklist to onboard
- Agent checklist after onboarding
- National, state and local compliance regulations
- Any additional documents needed for compliance

PARTNER ONBOARDING MANUAL / STEP BY STEP:

- **What:** Task to be completed
- **Who:** Person to complete onboarding task or portion of
- **When:** Phase/Section | onboarding [System]
- **Where:** Links or access to onboarding documents and materials
- **How:** Workflow Process Timing Compliance
- **Workflow:** List the workflow of each task or item for onboarding , and defining moments for tasks or items to be completed for agent, business, team, firm, or legal compliance
- **Communication:** Emails or communication guidelines for onboarding agents efficiently | Step by step

PHASE | STEP 1.

Introduction Agent Partnered | Sign Documents:

Business, Team, or Firm Roles and/or Responsibilities

Agent Roles / Responsibilities

Work-flow / Process Communication / Emails / Connections

Platform Links / Education Links

Documents / Attachments / Orientation Materials / Compliance

PHASE | STEP 2.

After Signing | During Transfer :

Business, Team, or Firm Roles and/or Responsibilities

Agent Roles / Responsibilities

Work-flow / Process Communication / Emails / Connections

Platform Links / Education Links

Documents / Attachments / Orientation Materials / Compliance

PHASE | STEP 3.

The Day of Transfer :

Business, Team, or Firm Roles and/or Responsibilities

Agent Roles / Responsibilities

Work-flow / Process Communication / Emails / Connections

Platform Links / Education Links

Documents / Attachments / Orientation Materials / Compliance

PHASE | STEP 4.

After Onboarding :

Business, Team, or Firm Roles and/or Responsibilities

Agent Roles / Responsibilities

Work-flow / Process Communication / Emails / Connections

Platform Links / Education Links

Documents / Attachments / Orientation Materials / Compliance

PHASE | STEPS [1-4] + SECTIONS [1-3] | EXAMPLE

Section 1 Firm Roles or Responsibilities | Agent Roles or Responsibilities
Work-flow / Process
Partners Onboarding manual | Step [1-4]
Section 2 Emails | Communication Links
Partners Onboarding manual | Step [1-4]
Section 3 Documents| Attachments

PHASE | STEP 1. [SECTION 1]:
Process | Agent Partnered | Sign Documents
Task | Action Items
Business, Team, or Firm Roles / Responsibilities
Agent Roles / Responsibilities
Workflow / Process

PHASE | STEP 1. [SECTION 2]:
Communication | Agent Partnered | Sign Documents
Attach all communication and connections [Attach Links]
Communication
Email Templates Guidelines - For Onboarding Staff / Agents
Document or Contract Explanations
Reference Information
Orientation Materials / Compliance Information
Platform Links / Education Links
Agent Links

PHASE | STEP 1. [SECTION 3]:
Documents | Agent Partnered | Sign Documents
Attach All Documents | Attachments for Step 1
Documents
Attachments
Guidelines

179

ONBOARDING PARTNERS MANUAL
MODULE 5 | SECTIONS 1-4
Conclusion

WRAP UP!

Partners Onboarding Manual Phase | Step [1-4]

- **Section 1**

Firm Roles or Responsibilities | Agent Roles or Responsibilities Workflow | Process

Partners Onboarding Manual Phase | Step [1-4]

- **Section 2**

Emails | Communication Links

Partners Onboarding Manual Phase | Step [1-4]

- **Section 3**

Documents | Attachments

ASK YOURSELF...

Introduction Agent Partnered / Sign Documents: The onboarding process should be clearly communicated. Will you onboard agents or staff in person or remotely?

After Signing / During Transfer : What tasks will the agent or staff member need to complete during onboarding? Will the new team member need to fill out paperwork, attend orientation sessions, training, and familiarize themselves with the business, team, or firm's policies, procedures, and systems?

The Day of Transfer : What is the local process to transfer listings? Will the agent need to sign documents on the day of transfer? What are the necessary steps that will need to take place for the business, team, firm, or the agent on the day of transfer?

After Onboarding : Have you created a list of items or tasks that will need to be completed, and instructions or compliance to complete, after onboarding? Including follow up, orientation, and education materials?

Agent Retention Plan : Who is responsible?

UREA RAPID
GROWTH MODEL

STEP BY STEP
PHASE 1-4

UREA
MODEL

- STEP 1 / START
- STEP 2 / BUILD
- STEP 3 / GROWTH
- STEP 4 / EXPANSION

UNIVERSAL REAL ESTATE AGENT RAPID GROWTH MODEL

Steps 1-4
Start - Expansion

This *Universal Real Estate Agent Operations Process Model* is meticulously designed to empower owners and entrepreneurs by providing a personalized framework that identifies critical holes and gaps in their business strategies. By taking a comprehensive approach, the model encourages individuals to assess their current operations, pinpoint areas that require improvement, and develop tailored solutions that align with their unique goals and aspirations. This process not only enhances operational efficiency but also fosters a deeper understanding of the business landscape, enabling agents to transition smoothly from their initial role as sales professionals to becoming effective business operators.

As agents evolve into business operators, they gain the skills necessary to manage teams, streamline processes, and implement strategic initiatives that drive growth. This model emphasizes the importance of *cultivating a strong foundation*, allowing entrepreneurs to refine their vision and establish best practices that support sustainable success. By focusing on personalized development, business owners can leverage their strengths, address weaknesses, and adopt innovative strategies that set them apart in a competitive market.

Ultimately, this framework serves as a *roadmap for real estate professionals* to progress from being agents to becoming fully-fledged business owners. By systematically addressing the challenges they face and creating actionable solutions, individuals can build a robust business that not only meets their immediate needs but also positions them for long-term success. This transformative journey empowers entrepreneurs to take control of their destinies, fostering a sense of ownership and accountability that is crucial for thriving in the ever-evolving world of business.

This rapid growth Model was crafted as a flexible framework, designed to guide you while inspiring *innovative thinking and creativity* in your approach. Rather than confining you to a rigid set of rules, this model encourages you to explore unique strategies that align with your individual strengths and market dynamics. It serves as a roadmap, *empowering* you to adapt and evolve your business practices to meet the ever-changing needs of your clients and the industry at large.

UREA RAPID GROWTH MODEL

Start:
Initially, you will seek to affiliate with a brokerage that aligns with your values, goals, and culture. This is where you will establish your foundation by sourcing partners, connections, and services that will support your business operations. It is essential to lay the groundwork for your business by building a network of trusted professionals and setting the stage for future growth.

Build:
During the build phase, you will start to construct your own personal business within the framework of your chosen brokerage, or build your own brokerage, and plan the direction of your business. This involves adding agents to your team, setting standards for performance and service, and identifying and filling any gaps in your operations. It is a critical phase where you establish your brand, define your value proposition, and create a solid infrastructure to support your growing business.

Growth:
As your business begins to gain traction in your local market, the growth phase focuses on expanding your reach, perfecting your standards, and optimizing your systems for maximum efficiency. This is a period of refining your processes, enhancing customer service, and solidifying your position as a trusted real estate business professional in your community. Once you have the systems in place, and you feel you have maximized your capabilities in your local market, it's time to expand!

Expansion:
In the final phase, you may choose to expand into other markets, leveraging your established partnerships, proven systems, and standards to maintain consistency, effectiveness, and efficiency across multiple locations. This phase involves scaling your business while ensuring that the quality of service and standards you have set remain consistent throughout your expansion efforts. Real estate agents can build, grow, and expand quickly in today's market with the proper use of technology.

START | GET CONNECTED!

JOINING A LARGE FIRM OR BROKER AS AN INDEPENDENT AGENT
Benefits:
- Access to training and resources: Large firms often provide extensive training programs and resources to help new agents get started in the industry.
- Brand recognition: Being associated with a well-known firm can help new agents establish credibility and attract clients.
- Independence: As an Independent Agent, you have the freedom to set your own schedule and work at your own pace.

Limitations:
- Competition: Large firms often have many agents competing for the same clients, making it harder for new agents to stand out.
- Fees and commission splits: Many large firms charge fees and take a percentage of commissions, which can eat into a new agent's earnings.
- Limited mentorship: While large firms may offer training, new agents may not receive personalized mentorship and support.

JOINING A TEAM UNDER A LARGE FIRM OR BROKER:
Benefits:
- Support and mentorship: Joining a team within a larger firm can provide new agents with valuable mentorship and support from experienced agents.
- Leads and referrals: Teams often have established networks and systems in place to generate leads and referrals for new agents.
- Collaboration: Working as part of a team allows new agents to collaborate with others, share resources, and learn from each other.

Limitations:
- Dependency: New agents may become overly reliant on the team for leads and support, limiting their independence and growth.
- Commission splits: Teams often have commission splits in place, meaning new agents may have to share a portion of their earnings with the team.
- Limited autonomy: Working as part of a team may restrict new agents' ability to make independent decisions about how they conduct business.

AFFILIATING WITH A SMALLER REAL ESTATE FIRM OR BROKERAGE

Affiliating with a smaller real estate firm or brokerage Is another option that new agents may consider when starting their career in real estate. Here are some pros and cons of affiliating with a smaller firm or brokerage:

Benefits:
- Personalized attention: Smaller firms and brokerages often provide more personalized attention and support to their agents, offering mentorship, guidance, and training tailored to individual needs.
- Flexibility: Smaller firms and brokerages may offer more flexibility in terms of commission, fees, and business practices, allowing agents to negotiate terms that work best for them.
- Tight-knit community: Working with a smaller firms and brokerages can create a sense of community and camaraderie among agents, fostering collaboration and a supportive work environment.
- Opportunities for growth: Smaller firms and brokerages may provide more opportunities for advancement and leadership roles, allowing agents to take on more responsibilities and grow within the company.

Limitations:
- Limited resources: Smaller firms and brokerages may have fewer resources and tools compared to larger firms and brokerages, which could impact an agent's ability to market properties, generate leads, or access advanced technology.
- Brand recognition: Smaller firms and brokerages may not have the same level of brand recognition or reputation as larger firms and brokerages, which could make it more challenging for agents to attract clients and compete in the market.
- Stability: Smaller firms and brokerages may be more vulnerable to market fluctuations and economic downturns, potentially impacting an agent's stability and income.
- Networking opportunities: Larger firms and brokerages often have a broader network of contacts and connections, which could provide agents with more opportunities for referrals and business growth.

CHOOSE WHERE TO START

Independence in the real estate industry comes with both responsibility and freedom, offering agents *opportunities for growth and success*. When deciding whether to affiliate as an independent broker/agent with a large firm, join a group or team under a large firm, or affiliate with a smaller firm or brokerage, it ultimately comes down to *personal preference* and individual goals. It is essential for real estate agents to carefully consider their options and interview with multiple brokerages before making a decision.

Affiliating as an independent broker with a large firm can provide access to a well-established brand, resources, and support, while still allowing for a certain level of autonomy and independence in running your business. Joining a group or team under a large firm can offer the benefits of a supportive network, training, and mentorship, while also providing opportunities for collaboration and shared resources. On the other hand, affiliating with a smaller firm can offer a more personalized and close-knit environment, with potentially more flexibility and individualized support.

Each real estate brokerage operates with its own *unique processes, systems, and leverage*, reflecting its distinct culture, values, and market strategies. As such, it is crucial for agents and entrepreneurs to conduct thorough research when selecting a brokerage that aligns with their personal and professional goals. Understanding the specific tools and support systems a brokerage offers can significantly impact your growth trajectory and overall success in the industry. By identifying a brokerage that resonates with your aspirations and provides the resources necessary for your development, you can establish a solid foundation from the start. This alignment not only enhances your ability to serve clients effectively but also fosters an environment conducive to personal growth.

By interviewing with multiple brokerages, agents can gain a better understanding of the culture, values, and resources offered by each firm, allowing them to make an informed decision that aligns with their professional goals and preferences. It is essential to ask questions, clarify expectations, and assess how well each brokerage can support your growth and success in the real estate industry. Ultimately, the choice of affiliation should be based on factors such as support, resources, culture, and opportunities for advancement that best fit your individual needs and future goals.

BUILD YOUR BUSINESS

CHOOSING TO OPEN YOUR OWN FIRM, OR BROKERAGE

Benefits:

- Complete control: Opening your own firm gives you complete control over your business operations, branding, and decision-making.
- Flexibility: You have the flexibility to set your own fees, commission structures, and business strategies.
- Unlimited growth potential: By opening your own firm, you have the potential to grow and expand your business as much as you desire.

Limitations:

- Increased responsibility: As a business owner , you will have increased responsibilities in terms of compliance, management, and financial oversight.
- Higher costs: Opening your own firm may require significant upfront investment in terms of licensing, insurance, office space, and marketing.
- Lack of brand recognition: Starting your own brokerage may require more effort to establish brand recognition and credibility in the market.

CHOOSING TO BUILD YOUR BUSINESS OR TEAM UNDER A
FRANCHISE OR LARGE FIRM:

Benefits:

- Brand recognition: Aligning with a well-known franchise or large firm can provide instant credibility and brand recognition in the market.
- Support and resources: Franchises and large firms often offer training, marketing support, and technology tools to help you grow your business.
- Established systems: Franchises typically have established systems and processes in place, making it easier for you to hit the ground running.

Limitations:

- Fees and royalties: Franchises typically require payment of fees and royalties, which can impact your bottom line.
- Limited autonomy: Working under a franchise may limit your autonomy and decision-making abilities in certain aspects of your business.
- Restrictions: Franchises may have specific guidelines and rules that you must follow, which could restrict your ability to operate independently.

GROW YOUR BUSINESS | MANAGE YOUR BUSINESS GROWTH

Ultimately, the decision to build your own team and develop your own brokerage in the future will depend on your *goals, preferences, and resources*. It is important to carefully weigh the benefits and limitations of each option through growth and consider how they align with your short-term and long-term business objectives.

When building a real estate business, you have the flexibility create your own leadership team if you feel it is necessary for the growth and success of your company. By hiring leaders with a *diverse set of skills* that complement your own, who are knowledgeable, and have practical experience in the real estate industry, you can set your business up for success. Here are some key points to consider when building a leadership team:

Diverse Skill Set: Look for leaders who bring different skills and expertise to the table. For example, if you excel in sales and marketing, consider hiring a leader who is strong in operations or finance to balance out the team.

Practical Experience: Leaders who have practical experience in the real estate industry can provide valuable insights and guidance based on their own experiences. This can help you navigate challenges, make informed decisions, and drive growth.

Connection and Relatability: Effective leadership is not just about skills and experience; it also involves building connections and establishing relatability with your team. Leaders who can connect with employees on a personal level, understand their needs and motivations, and create a positive work environment, can inspire loyalty and drive performance.

Setting a Vision: Your leadership team should be aligned with your vision and values for the business. By setting a clear vision and direction for the company, you can ensure that everyone is working towards a common goal and driving the business forward together.

Communication and Collaboration: Strong leadership involves effective communication and collaboration. Encourage open communication, feedback, and collaboration among leaders and team members to foster a culture of transparency, trust, and teamwork.

By building a strong leadership team with diverse skills, practical experience, and a shared vision, you can set your real estate business up for long-term success and growth. Effective leadership through connection and relatability can inspire and motivate your team, drive performance, and create a positive culture.

MANAGE YOUR PARTNERSHIPS AND CONNECTIONS

By hiring specific partners who excel in *performing specialized tasks or services*, you can scale your real estate business rapidly and strategically. Partnering with individuals or companies that bring unique skills, expertise, and resources to the table can help you expand your business, reach a broader audience, and increase efficiency. Here are some key benefits of hiring specific partners to scale your business:

Expertise: Partnering with professionals who specialize in areas such as marketing, technology, finance, or operations can bring valuable expertise to your business. Their specialized knowledge and skills can help you address complex challenges, implement best practices, and capitalize on new opportunities.

Efficiency: By delegating specific tasks or services to partners who are experts in their field, you can streamline your operations and improve efficiency. This allows you to focus on your core strengths and strategic priorities while leveraging the capabilities of your partners to drive growth.

Scalability: Partnering with specialized partners enables you to scale your business more rapidly and effectively. Whether you need to expand into new markets, launch new services, or handle increased demand, having the right partners in place can help you grow your business in a sustainable and scalable manner.

Flexibility: Hiring specific partners gives you the flexibility to access resources and capabilities on an as-needed basis. This allows you to adapt to changing market conditions, seize new opportunities, and respond to challenges without the need for extensive internal resources or infrastructure.

Innovation: Collaborating with partners who bring fresh perspectives, ideas, and approaches to the table can drive innovation within your business. By fostering a culture of collaboration and creativity, you can stay ahead of the competition and differentiate your brand in the market.

Hiring specific partners to perform specialized tasks or services can be a strategic approach to scaling your real estate business rapidly and with precision. By leveraging the expertise, efficiency, scalability, flexibility, and innovation that partners bring, you can position your business for long-term success and sustainable growth.

MANAGE YOUR LEADERSHIP

As you grow your real estate business and transition from handling day-to-day tasks to focusing on strategic growth and leadership, it becomes essential to have solid support, reliable partners, and a strong infrastructure in place to properly support your business through its expansion. Having a team that is working to *support the vision* is an important factor in sustaining consistency through growth and expansion. Here are some key considerations to keep in mind as you navigate this phase of growth:

Establish a Strong Leadership Team: Surround yourself with a competent and reliable leadership team that can help drive the business forward, manage operations effectively, and make strategic decisions in your absence.

Delegate Responsibilities: Delegate tasks and responsibilities to capable team members or partners, allowing you to focus on high-level strategic initiatives and business development opportunities.

Build Strong Partnerships: Collaborate with trusted partners, such as vendors, service providers, and industry professionals, who can support your business operations and contribute to its success.

Implement Efficient Systems and Processes: Streamline your business operations by implementing efficient systems and processes that can help improve productivity, reduce inefficiencies, and ensure smooth workflow.

Invest in Technology: Utilize technology tools and platforms to automate routine tasks, enhance communication, and improve the overall efficiency of your business operations.

Focus on Professional Development: Invest in the ongoing training and development of your team members to ensure they have the skills and knowledge needed to support the growth and success of the business.

Maintain a Strong Company Culture: Foster a positive company culture that promotes teamwork, collaboration, and mutual respect among employees, creating a supportive and productive work environment.

Monitor Performance and Results: Regularly track and analyze key performance indicators to assess the effectiveness of your business strategies, identify areas for improvement, and make data-driven decisions.

MANAGE YOUR MARKETING

1. Digital Marketing: This includes managing social media accounts, running online advertising campaigns, and creating digital content to promote listings and attract clients.

2. Website Development and Maintenance: Having a professional website is essential for showcasing listings, providing information to clients, and generating leads. This task may require the expertise of web developers and designers.

3. Search Engine Optimization (SEO): Optimizing your website and online content for search engines can help improve your visibility and ranking in search results. SEO specialists can help with keyword research, content optimization, and link building.

4. Graphic Design: Creating visually appealing marketing materials such as flyers, brochures, and presentations can enhance your branding and attract potential clients. Graphic designers can help with designing and producing these materials.

5. Photography and Videography: High-quality photos and videos are crucial for showcasing properties and attracting buyers. Hiring professional photographers and videographers can help you create compelling visual content.

6. Copywriting: Crafting engaging property descriptions, blog posts, and marketing materials requires strong writing skills. Copywriters can help you create compelling and persuasive content that resonates with your target audience.

7. Email Marketing: Building and maintaining an email list, creating email campaigns, and analyzing performance metrics are all tasks that can be outsourced to email marketing specialists.

8. Public Relations: Building relationships with the media, securing press coverage, and managing your public image can be handled by PR professionals who specialize in real estate.

9. Event Planning: Hosting open houses, client appreciation events, and networking functions requires coordination and planning. Event planners can help you organize and execute successful events.

10. Market Research: Understanding market trends, analyzing data, and identifying opportunities for growth require research skills. Hiring market research analysts can help you make informed decisions and stay ahead of the competition.

MANAGE YOUR AGENT AND CLIENT RELATIONSHIPS

By *delegating* these customer relationship management tasks to assistants, employees or partners with the necessary skills and expertise, real estate agents and business owners can focus on building strong client relationships, delivering exceptional service, and growing their business.

Lead Generation and Prospecting: Identifying and reaching out to potential clients through various channels such as social media, email marketing, and networking events.

Client Onboarding: Managing the process of welcoming new clients, gathering necessary information, and setting expectations for the relationship.

Customer Communications: Maintaining regular communication with clients through phone calls, emails, newsletters, and other channels to provide updates, answer questions, and address concerns.

Database Management: Organizing and maintaining client information, interactions, and preferences in a centralized database for easy access and reference.

Follow-Up and Follow-Through: Ensuring timely follow-up on client inquiries, requests, and feedback to provide excellent customer service and build strong relationships.

Client Feedback and Satisfaction: Gathering feedback from clients on their experience, satisfaction levels, and areas for improvement to enhance service quality and client retention.

Client Events and Engagement: Planning and organizing client appreciation events, workshops, seminars, and other engagement activities to foster relationships and add value to clients.

Referral Management: Implementing strategies to encourage and track client referrals, rewarding clients for referrals, and leveraging referral networks to expand the client base.

Customer Support and Issue Resolution: Addressing client inquiries, concerns, and issues promptly and effectively to ensure a positive customer experience and maintain client loyalty.

Client Education and Resources: Providing clients with relevant information, resources, and educational materials to help them make informed decisions and navigate the real estate process successfully.

MANAGE YOUR DOCUMENTS AND CLIENT RELATIONSHIPS

In real estate, a transaction coordinator or specialist often plays a crucial role in managing the *administrative aspects of a transaction*, such as paperwork, deadlines, and communication between parties. In addition to these responsibilities, some transaction coordinators or specialists may also take on marketing and customer relationship management tasks for agents. The services offered in this capacity can vary depending on the coordinator or specialist's skills, experience, and expertise. Below are some task or services you may want or need to outsource, for your team or your business, before or during expansion.

1.**Transaction Coordination:** Managing and coordinating the various documents and tasks involved in real estate transactions, ensuring all parties are informed and deadlines are met.

2.**Marketing Collateral Creation:** Designing and producing marketing materials such as brochures, flyers, and advertisements to promote properties and attract buyers.

3.**Client Communication:** Maintaining regular communication with clients, providing updates on listings, scheduling showings, and addressing inquiries and concerns.

4.**Listing Management:** Uploading and managing property listings on multiple platforms, ensuring accuracy and consistency in property information.

5.**Market Research:** Conducting research on local real estate market trends, property values, and competition to inform pricing strategies and marketing efforts.

6.**Property Inspections:** Coordinating and scheduling property inspections, reviewing inspection reports, and addressing any issues or concerns raised.

7.**Legal Document Preparation:** Completing and reviewing legal documents such as purchase agreements, contracts, and disclosures to ensure compliance with regulations and protect clients' interests.

8.**Financial Analysis:** Analyzing financial data, such as property values, market trends, and investment opportunities, to provide clients with informed recommendations and guidance.

9.**Open House Coordination:** Planning and organizing open houses, coordinating schedules, preparing marketing materials, and managing visitor interactions.

10.**Client Relationship Management:** Building and maintaining relationships with clients, providing personalized service, and addressing their needs and preferences throughout the buying or selling process.

UNIVERSAL LAW OF UNITY:

UNDERSTANDING THE INTERCONNECTEDNESS OF ALL PEOPLE FOSTERS A SENSE OF COMMUNITY IN YOUR BUSINESS EFFORTS. BY PRIORITIZING COLLABORATION AND RELATIONSHIP-BUILDING, YOU CREATE A SUPPORTIVE NETWORK THAT ENHANCES YOUR ABILITY TO SERVE CLIENTS. THIS INTERCONNECTED APPROACH STRENGTHENS YOUR BUSINESS FOUNDATION, PROMOTING MUTUAL GROWTH AND SUCCESS IN THE REAL ESTATE INDUSTRY.

EXPAND YOUR BUSINESS

Expansion teams can offer several benefits to business owners in the real estate Industry, but they also come with limitations. Here are some of the key benefits and limitations of expansion teams:

Benefits:
- Increased market reach: Expansion teams allow business owners to tap into new markets and reach a larger audience of potential clients.
- Scalability: By establishing expansion teams in different locations, business owners can scale their operations and grow their business more rapidly.
- Enhanced brand recognition: Expansion teams can help increase brand visibility and recognition in multiple markets, strengthening the overall brand presence.
- Diversification: Having expansion teams in different locations can help diversify the business and reduce dependency on a single market.
- Access to local expertise: Expansion teams can provide business owners with access to local knowledge and expertise, helping them navigate specific market conditions and trends.

Limitations:
- Management challenges: Managing multiple expansion teams can be complex and time-consuming, requiring effective communication, coordination, and oversight.
- Quality control: Ensuring consistent quality of service across all expansion teams can be challenging, especially when teams are located in different markets.
- Cost considerations: Establishing and maintaining expansion teams in different locations can be costly, requiring investment in resources, infrastructure, and support.
- Risk of misalignment: There is a risk of misalignment between the business owner's vision and goals and the operations of the expansion teams, leading to potential conflicts and inefficiencies.
- Legal and regulatory complexities: Operating expansion teams in different locations may involve navigating various legal and regulatory requirements, which can add complexity and compliance challenges.
- Expansion teams can be a strategic growth opportunity for business owners. With the use of technology, shared resources, and national partnerships, we can now easily mitigate many of the limitations.

01.

STEP 1.
START

AFFILIATE | GET STARTED!
Get familiar with your systems | Build your foundation
- Customer Relationship Management [CRM]
- Marketing
- Transaction Coordination | Documents
- Lead Generation | Networking
- Set Goals | Create a process and plan to achieve

02.

STEP 2.
BUILD

Construct | Assess your systems
Build a solid infrastructure
- Customer Relationship Management [CRM]
- Marketing
- Transaction Coordination | Documents
- Lead Generation | Networking
- Add services, partners, or agents that align with your vision

03.

STEP 3.
GROWTH

Maximize your local market
- Refine your systems
- Optimize your process | Systems
- Enhance customer service
- Identify, assess, and network your expansion market
- Integrate any technology or national partners for expansion

04.

STEP 4.
EXPANSION

Expand and scale your business
- Source any local partners needed in your expansion market
- Use your trusted partners to expand your brand
- Maintain consistency through expansion
- Maximize your expansion market
- Identify, assess, and network your next expansion market

MODULE 1. Step-by-step business operations manual: This comprehensive guide outlines the *core operations, processes, and procedures* of your real estate business. It includes information on administrative tasks, financial management, marketing strategies, client communication protocols, and other essential aspects of running your business. Having a well-documented business operations manual ensures consistency, efficiency, and scalability as you expand your business.

MODULE 2. Step-by-step sellers agent manual: This manual provides detailed instructions and best practices for *agents working with sellers*. It covers the listing process, property marketing strategies, pricing strategies, negotiation techniques, and closing procedures. By equipping your agents with a structured guide, you can ensure that they follow a standardized approach and deliver high-quality service to sellers.

MODULE 3. Step-by-step buyers agent manual: Similar to the seller's agent manual, this guide offers step-by-step instructions for *agents working with buyers*. It includes information on the home buying process, market analysis, property search strategies, offer preparation, contract negotiation, and closing procedures. Providing agents with a clear roadmap for working with buyers helps them deliver a seamless and professional experience to clients.

MODULE4. Step-by-step gaining partners manual: This guide outlines the criteria, process, and strategies for *recruiting and selecting strategic partners* to support your real estate business. It includes tips for identifying potential partners, evaluating their qualifications, negotiating agreements, and establishing productive working relationships. By following a structured recruiting guide, and creating a partner packet to showcase value, you can build a network of reliable and competent partners to enhance your business operations and services.

MODULE 5. Step-by-step onboarding partners manual: A *comprehensive onboarding process* is crucial for integrating new agents into your team effectively. This step-by-step guide covers orientation, training, mentorship, goal-setting, performance evaluation, and ongoing support for new agents. By providing a structured onboarding program, you can help agents acclimate to your business culture, standards, and practices, setting them up for success in their roles.

By implementing these five essential modules from the *Universal Real Estate Agent Model,* you can establish a strong foundation for your business, empower your team to excel, and navigate growth and expansion with confidence and consistency!

CONNECT DIRECTLY OR JOIN OUR COMMUNITY :

UniversalBrokerSolutions.com

DEDICATION:

To my fellow builders, entrepreneur's, realtors, and those of you behind the scenes, scavenging the pieces and parts of a business to make it whole, turning the dream into a reality, and bringing the vision to life, the world is not possible without you. Keep digging, keep building, and most importantly continue to actively, intentionally, and continuously create the world you want to live in.

www.ingramcontent.com/pod-product-compliance
Lightning Source LLC
Chambersburg PA
CBHW080612270326
41928CB00016B/3015